# Change Your Conversation...Change Your Life

## Building Bigger Better Boxes

### By John D. Knight

First Edition 2001
Second Printing 2003
Third Printing 2005

Life is for Living Publications, Inc.
San Diego, California

First Published in 2001 by
Life is for Living, Inc.
Atlanta, Georgia

First Edition
Second Printing
Third Printing

All Rights Reserved
Copyright © 2001 John Knight. All rights reserved. No part
of this book may be used or reproduced in any manner
whatsoever without the written permission from the author,
except in the inclusion of brief quotations in a review.

ISBN 0-9706817-3-9

Printed in the United States of America

You may Contact the Author at:
BigBoxJohn@Yahoo.com
Or
www.johnknight.cc
or
John Knight
PO Box 632816
San Diego, CA  92163

This book is dedicated to my parents, Mom & Jim, Dad & Linda, who have lovingly supported and encouraged my well being, happiness, and success throughout my life.

# Acknowledgments

Some very dear friends took time to encourage and love me through this process. Thank you to the following for the suggestions and edits to the early manuscript: Alyse Praytor, Sue McGinnis, Ellie Harold, and Sue Moore. Much appreciation to David Greenberg for setting the example of what it is to be a successful national speaker and author. Special thanks go to my good friend Dennis Wholey for the dinner in Georgetown where the desire for this book came together as a reality. To each of you I give a hug and a prayer.

# Table of Contents

# Introduction
## From John

The quest for self-improvement happened early in my life. I always knew there was a better way to live and a better way to do things. As a child I remember working on my bike to make it faster and made it look a little better with daily cleanings. Since then, my life has been transformed by what I believe to be the most important idea in any language. "There must be a better way."

This idea has led people throughout the ages to find cures for supposedly incurable diseases, to create better modes of transportation, and to build better relationships with those they love. Every human being strives for something better in their life. We need knowledge, information, and, very importantly, we need tools. This book contains all three.

My early twenties found me steeped in alcoholism and depression. Some very compassionate people reached out to help me get sober. I thought all I needed was to quit drinking. They had a better idea for me. After helping me get sober, they showed me how to change my life by changing my thoughts and actions, one day at a time.

This process helped me transform my life. It included taking an inventory of myself, cleaning up my past mistakes, doing forgiveness work, and being of service to other people in the world. I realized that when I changed the way I thought, talked, and acted, my life became richer. My hope is you can learn to apply the incredible lessons in this book to uplift your life as I have. May God bless you on your life's journey as God has blessed me.

# Chapter 1
# **Creative Conversations**

## How Life Works
People glow excitedly at the thought of success. The idea of success means different things to different people. For one person it may mean financial wealth and to another it may mean great radiant health, physical strength and or endurance. To another person, it may mean having a harmonious family and home where compassion and loyalty thrive. The one truth each and every person must respect is that everyone must take responsibility for creating their own life experience, especially in regards to success.

It is through your conversations that you create your life. And it is through your conversations, balanced with your thoughts and daily actions, that you direct your life. This book is about looking at your conversations, thoughts, and actions. What you think and what you verbalize are the elements leading to your actions. For actions to change there must be a change in thought and belief. Change your conversations and you change your life.

## Language is the Key
Thoughts and beliefs are the fundamental elements for each one of us to transform our lives and they are rooted in language. Language is the key element in your life. Without language you would have a difficult time communicating or thinking. Communication and language are your tools in being a creative force in your life. These tools are vital for your successes and need to be used with an attentive mind. Everyone creates their life with their conversations. There are two types of conversations: conversations that you have with yourself (thinking), and conversations you have with others. Of course, we use

language as the main component in our communications. You also use non-verbal communication.

Take a deeper look at language. It gives you a tool that allows you to communicate your dreams, feelings, and ideas. It works wonderfully well in these areas. On the other hand, language also limits everything through its use. Language sets boundaries in a limitless universe. These limits and boundaries may not be clear to you. Take a look at the following example.

To set a goal of living in a twenty room mansion is a limitation. Why not a thirty-room mansion? While a twenty-room mansion may be quite large it is still limited to being only twenty rooms. While the universe is unlimited, you live in a world limited by language. We need to put limitations on our experiences to define them. This is not necessarily bad. It depends on how we do it. We live in a world where our limitations can be huge.

## Using Language
We use language to create boundaries, borders, and walls. Any boundary is a limitation, no matter how large. As an example, let's say your salary is currently $3,000.00 a month and you set a goal of $25,000.00 a month. This is a clearly defined goal and immensely bigger than your current salary. The goal of the larger salary, while tremendous, still has a limit or boundary attached to it. This goal creates a border or wall that is quite comfortable compared to your current salary; however, it is still a boundary and limitation. In essence, all language creates a box defined by boundaries, borders, and walls. The box, as it will be referred to throughout this book, is created by the words you use in your thinking and spoken language.

## You Live in a Box

Motivational speakers, authors and business leaders often use buzz phrases in their communications. A number of years ago the buzz phrase being used was "paradigm shift". I am not so sure how many people really knew what it meant, but everybody pounced on it. Today there is a popular buzz phrase that says, "You gotta get outside your box."

The truth is you cannot get outside of your box. How can I assert such a negative statement? Well, we need to look at what a box is. A box is simply the world you live in based on your beliefs, attitudes, perceptions, and conversations. Basically, you and I create a box called "our lives". While reading this book, it will be useful if you could imagine yourself being in a box. Sometimes being in a big box. Sometimes being in a small box.

Being in a box is not necessarily unsound, unless it is a small, uncomfortable, limited box created by negative, limited conversations that are based on limiting beliefs. You will be invited in this book to look at the box you have created for yourself and begin to build it in ways that are pleasing and empowering. I encourage you to change some of your beliefs, especially the negative ones, and build a more positive life.

You create a box for yourself every time you use language to speak or think. Speaking and thinking is based on language, which puts boundaries and limits on your world. Language does this so you can understand and make sense of your world.

You use words verbally or in thought, and by their nature, words define and outline your life. These words create the box you live in. Some big. Some small. This is what it is to be a human being. To put this simply, the box is defined as the expanded or limited way you live based on your beliefs and conversations. Your beliefs are communicated to others, as well as yourself, mostly through the medium of language.

## Belief System
All of your thinking and all of your conversations originate from your belief system, especially the beliefs you hold about yourself. If you think that you are a courageous person, then you hold within yourself a positive belief which creates a large box in which you live. On the opposite side, you have some negative beliefs that influence you in building small boxes to live in. Examples of adverse beliefs are: I am not good enough, I am too fat, I am not smart enough, I don't have enough money. Remember, you are always in a box, big or small.

The beliefs you hold about the world affect you in ways you may or may not yet understand. It is time to link your belief system with the concept of the box. The more optimistic, positive and goal oriented your beliefs, the bigger and more expanded the box you live in. The more limited, negative, and pessimistic you see yourself or the world, the smaller the box you live in.

The box you live in can be very large and wonderful or it can be small and confining. It is your choice and you are creating it everyday through your conversations. This is great news for you! If you want to live an amazing life, then build a huge box to live in. As you change your conversations and thoughts, you will be motivated to new actions and your life will change.

## Box Building

You create the box either big or small on a daily basis by your conversations, thoughts, and beliefs. Limitations are created by your thoughts and beliefs, which create the boundaries you live within life. Even the biggest goals you set for yourself have limits and boundaries. This does not mean that you should not set goals. Successful people know the magnitude and importance of setting goals. They set them big enough to build really big boxes to live in. Big goals, like living in a twenty-room mansion or a salary of $25,000.00 a month.

Positive thinking has nothing to do with magically creating wonderful things out of thin air. Your conversations are not magical and have nothing to do with enchanted words. Using your conversations to build big boxes is simply using positive words to change the way you feel and to shift your attitude to a more positive one.

This book and its teachings are based on a favorite scripture from the New Testament. "...be ye transformed by the renewing of your mind..." Romans 12:2. Renewing your mind is proactively changing your thinking. The power of positive thinking has been around for many years and has been successfully used by countless numbers of people to change their lives for the better. God wants good for each and every one of us. It is up to us to have better thoughts and beliefs to create a better life.

Nobody can think for you and nobody can change your thinking. You are the only one who is in charge of your thinking. Are you ready to take charge and think differently so that you can live differently?

## Limited Beliefs

A term that will be used in this book is limited belief. A limited belief is one that keeps you from obtaining, being, or having something you desire in your life. Examples are: I am too old to get a good job, good companies don't hire people unless they have a degree, I don't have enough time, and I don't have enough talent.

These types of beliefs become the walls and boundaries of the very small boxes that we build and then must live in. Limiting beliefs seem very real when we believe them. The reason they seem so real is that we look to the outside world for facts and not to the creative desire we have within us by looking at what is possible. The fact the stock market is going down has very little to do with your potential to be financially rich. Your being rich must be grounded in the belief that you can build financial wealth.

Concentrating on the limitations of the outside world solves few problems. Focusing on the desired result, which is not currently seen by the naked eye, is what solves problems. This is where faith comes in.

Can you imagine a person looking for a job with the mindset that nobody wants to hire someone over the age of forty? Every time they begin to look for work, the underlying belief is that they are not going to be wanted. With this limited belief, they are creating an attitude of rejection, which sends out a non-verbal signal. The employers can somehow pick up on the negativity and may find reasons not to hire them. People intuitively pick up on each other's beliefs and attitudes. While the person may have truly wanted the job, the underlying belief is somehow what comes through. Beliefs create conversations, attitudes, actions, thinking, feelings, and more beliefs that can actually be seen by others.

Also, people make up stories based on their limited beliefs. They tell others their limitations (justifications). 'Well, I could have a better position in this company, but the managers want to promote someone who has a college degree. Since I never got a promotion to make more money, I couldn't afford to attend college, which is so expensive. It is just a catch-22. Seems like I just can't win.' Can you see how limiting these conversations can be? They justify the underlying limited belief so the person can shrug off responsibility for the outcome.

You and I both know that if someone really wanted to attend college they could. But ask the person telling the story and they will come up with twenty excuses. These excuses will seem justifiable and plausible as to why they can't go to college. All the excuses will sound good and they will argue for their limitations until they are blue in the face. Every excuse, no matter how valid it may seem, is a conversation that creates and supports living in a small and limited box. I love the wise philosophy that is so true: "Argue for your limitations and you get them." Your conversations and thoughts are very powerful in creating your day to day life experience.

## It is Just a Thought
The essence of all language is the ability to organize and deliver your thought process through conversations. This creates your beliefs and feelings. Thoughts are formulated in your brain by sending a minuscule amount of electricity along the pathways in your brain to be stored as a belief. It is amazing how such a diminutive amount of energy can

impact your life so powerfully. Thoughts and beliefs have a huge impact on your daily life.

Right now, as you read this, take a moment to do the following exercise. The exercise will only take about a minute and will help you connect the teaching of this book to your everyday life.

For the next fifteen seconds think about someone in the past with whom you feel angry or someone who deeply wronged you. Get into the emotion of how you felt. Check out your physiology. How does your body feel when you think and feel about this angry and hurtful situation?

Now, for fifteen seconds, think about someone you love. Think of a romantic or pleasant time when you were together. Make this memory vivid with details. Notice what kind of feelings come over you. See if your physiology changes. As you stop for a moment and do these things, take note of how you begin to feel.

By now you are certainly beginning to understand how your thoughts and emotions are linked. They work hand in hand. If a person does not use their authority when controlling their thinking, their thinking can take them to places they may prefer not to go emotionally.

## What Do You Want?
You picked this book up for a reason. No doubt you want something more in your life. You may want more abundance, deep job satisfaction, exotic vacations, or more time to spend with your family.

The basic principle of this book is "Change your thoughts and you change your life" or, to put it another way,

"Thinking is a creative process." Great teachers and philosophers have taught this. Positive thinking can create experiences of happiness, joy, fulfillment, and love. The result of negative thinking is tension, stress, anger, and fear. Thinking works both ways. Have you begun to notice the truth of this in your own life?

This is not about being "Pollyanna" or blindly optimistic. While optimism plays a vital role in living successfully, it is not meant to keep your head in the clouds about real life situations. Part of changing your belief system is learning to interpret facts in ways that do not shrink your box. If you are going through a health challenge, then by all means don't pretend you aren't. Just don't focus all of your energy or conversation on the illness. Focus on getting well.

Use the wisdom and intelligence God gave you and do the necessary activities to get well. First of all, convince yourself that you can get well. Conceive that getting well is possible. Then be willing to do whatever it takes to get well. Stop telling people about how sick you are, how hard it is to get well, or any statistic the medical community has given you. Do not believe the percentages that the news and television advertisements give in regards to health and sickness. There are always exceptions to these awful statistics, and you can be that exception.

Your conversations and thoughts need to be on health and healing. People do not get well by thinking about how sick they are. People do not get well by telling all their friends and family members about how their chances don't look too bright. People do not get well by focusing on the negative. They get well because of the idea of health and healing. Find a medical, health, or spiritual practitioner that truly believes you can get well. The conversations you have with them must be based on the belief in your healing. Talking of negativity by you or anyone else creates a small box for healing. You want and deserve to live a healthy life in a big box.

Again, be honest about your situation, but look at what is possible and focus on that. If you are having financial problems, then take an honest look at how much money you owe. Put it on paper. Most people will keep their "head in the sand" and not take an honest look. For many it may seem too big or difficult to comprehend their actual debt. But, the light must be shined on the problem to dissipate it. The truth must be seen in its entirety and then you can begin to find ways of paying off the debt in a responsible manner. You can get out of debt. It may take some serious work and effort. Establish the belief that it is possible and focus on ways to clear the debts.

### Comfort Zones
Let us revisit the buzz phrase "You gotta get outside your box." This is said over and over with little regard to what is really meant. The phrase really means that a person must get outside their Comfort Zone, or to say it more plainly, to get out of the rut of negative, self-limiting thinking. This getting out of negative ruts would include stopping old habits, fear, negative thoughts, and pessimism.

There is a big difference between getting outside the box (which is impossible) and getting outside the Comfort Zone. A Comfort Zone is a place where you feel safe, familiar, comfortable, and often stagnant. It is a place where you do not have to risk much in life. Keeping a ship in a harbor will keep the ship safe from being battered by the sea. Staying in the harbor does not allow the ship do what it was built to do, which is taking adventurous souls to sea.

Risk little and receive little. When you risk little and stay safe in life, there is minimal growth and little expansive living. Old habits, limiting thoughts, and fear create comfort zones which limit the possibility of living an amazing life.

Some people find it difficult to talk with strangers. It is not that they are unable; they just experience excessive amounts of fear and anxiety. These feelings are the result of some form of a limited belief.

What kind of belief might a person have that would cause them to be uncomfortable talking with strangers? It could be a belief that strangers are dangerous. Maybe a person perceives that they will be judged as nosy or pushy. They may fear being rejected. Such beliefs are usually learned from early childhood or in school.

Successful salespeople overcome these types of limited beliefs. Initially, they endure the uneasy feelings of talking with strangers. But, as time goes on, they find that in making cold calls they have not died or bled to death. They realize it is not so bad and can do it without great suffering. With repeated experience, a new belief is established. They begin to live from a new belief system. This is "getting outside their comfort zone." pushing the boundaries, and CREATING A BIGGER BOX. Getting out of a comfort zone simply means doing an activity that is advantageous to you but feels uncomfortable doing.

### Quick!  Get Out Now
Another example of getting outside the comfort zone is when the training wheels are taken off a child's bike. Great fear is felt by the child when their parent suggests it is time to take the training wheels off their bike. The child cannot

imagine how they could ride the bike without them. The belief that they will be unable to ride without the training wheels is a small box belief that limits the child's biking experience. At some point, the wheels need to come off. The child hesitates and begs to keep them attached to the bike. The loving parent assures them that they can ride without the aid of the training wheels. At first, it might be a scary experience accompanied by falls and the inability to balance. Yet, ultimately, the child will gain freedom and adventure.

The parent is probably pretty confident that the child is ready for this next step or they would not have suggested it. In this example, the parent has a belief in the child's ability (this parent is holding a big box for the child). At this point the child is living in the small box belief that they cannot do it. If the child trusts the parent, they will begin to expand their small box by becoming more willing to try riding without the training wheels. Eventually, the child will take on the big box belief offered by the parent.

It would be great if the child did this quickly with little resistance. But we know crying and begging will be part of the process of learning. None of us like letting go of something we find safe and familiar. Hopefully the parent is gentle, encouraging, and persistent with this new riding option. Like it or not, many of us are not joyfully welcoming of things new and different. When we resist life and the constant change it offers, we shrink our box.

Eventually we do grow and evolve. Do you remember getting past the training wheels and finally riding your bike? You felt joy in riding to places that you found adventurous and delighted in the extreme ecstasy of speeding down a steep hill. You were able to be in control of your bike and command it in the direction you wanted to go. You could feel the sunshine on your face and the wind in your hair. The doubt seemed so long ago and far away. What a vivid example of how life really works. Why do we resist change so fervently only to break through a short time later, forgetting the doubt we had adamantly clung to?

Coming to believe you could ride the bike without the training wheels and then actually doing it is how to build a BIGGER box for yourself. We took so many more risks as children. Living on the edge! Oh, the thrill of living on the edge! It should not have been lost in childhood.

### See the Truth
Do you remember lying in bed at night paralyzed by the thought there was a monster under your bed? What fear and worry you created. Of course, there was no monster, but it sure felt real to you at the time. In that moment your thoughts created a small cramped box based purely on your faulty thought process – called fantasy. You created a negative fantasy.

You had a conversation with yourself, which continued to lead you down the road of dread and horror, until one of your parents came in and turned on the light.

Your parent may have held your hand while you both looked under the bed with the light turned on. There was no monster under the bed. You took this new fact and created a new belief. Your parent simply showed you a new way of looking at the situation where you could make up a new belief that no monster existed. With no monster under the bed, you created a bigger box for yourself — a box of safety and security.

A little later in the night, maybe the old thought reoccurred and you began to believe that the monster was under the bed again. The fear and worry returned. Or maybe the fear never quite left and the negative feelings began to dictate your thoughts, which slammed you back into the images of the monster. In this instance, it happens so quickly that it would be hard to distinguish which came first, the feeling of fear or the thought of the monster. In the very beginning the thought definitely created the fear. Then the two, working together, spiraled you out of control.

Your thinking is the key here. A monster under the bed equaled a small box filled with fear. No monster under the bed equaled a big box where you felt safe.

Since there is no monster, it could not affect the size of your box. There was only the self-generated belief of a monster. For a child, as well as an adult, this type of thinking has a powerful effect on our emotions. Boxes are built solely on the beliefs that you hold in your mind. A box is created no matter how unfounded or crazy the belief, or even if the perceived belief is real or not. Thinking creates beliefs and beliefs make up the box – big or small. And you live in a self created box.

## The Flexibility of the Box

The box you live in is not static or fixed. As a matter of fact, it grows and shrinks all the time. From big to small, and/or vice-versa. Think of a box with moveable walls, a box that expands and contracts. This flexing and stretching is directly related to your positive or negative thinking and speaking. It is also responds to your confidence and willingness to see life's possibilities.

The box has walls like rubber bands. The walls expand and contract many times every day depending on how much you stay focused on the positive or negative. One moment you are talking with a friend about a new business idea which will help many people. Your box is huge. This is the business you have always dreamed of; doing work that will bring you great joy and will afford you a good living. As you continue talking, you find yourself eager and enthusiastic. The more possibilities you think of, the bigger your box gets.

How do you know you have a big box in this moment? Simple, you feel good. You are focused on good outcomes. You are optimistic. Your energy is high. A smile is plastered on your face.

All of a sudden you begin to think of all the bookkeeping you must do for the business. Here comes the shrinking of your box. You tell yourself how much you despise paperwork and keeping records. Details have never been your thing. You begin to talk about how hard this might be; how your business might fail. You begin to worry. Your friend begins to sympathize. All of a sudden your new business prospect does not seem like such a good idea. You feel overwhelmed. Your box begins to shrink even more. You have just taken yourself from a big wonderful box to a small box in a matter of minutes.

Your friend cheerfully says she knows of a great accountant who is just starting a business and has reasonable prices. Your eyes light up and you ask if he might take you on as a new client. Now you are back into possibilities. Your box is growing. You are feeling optimistic again. Wow, the accountant idea is going to work. The box has expanded.

This is a brief example of how your box can grow and shrink again and again during the day, all by the thoughts and conversations you have with yourself and others. It is your job to watch your conversations carefully and use them responsibly. Change your thoughts and conversations, and your life will change. Take charge of your thoughts and your box grows larger. Thoughts and conversations are powerful in their effect on us.

## Boxes & Money
Your beliefs, conscious and unconscious, are the raw ingredients of your box. Thinking of shortcomings or disaster leaves few options and the effect is a limited life – a small boxed life.

Believing one cannot do a certain thing because he or she has no money has stopped too many people from having the life they desire and deserve. They may dream, but deep down they believe in limitation and insufficiency.

I met a man who had very little money, but for years dreamed of going on a cruise. He had a hard time making ends meet and, needless to say, there never seemed to be enough money for something as extravagant as a cruise. He did a wise thing over the years. He kept his box big by keeping the cruise in the back of his mind. His dreams were filled with thoughts of what he might experience on a cruise and all the exotic ports of call. He felt discouraged at times but stayed optimistic and open to the possibility of going on a cruise. Yet for many years, there was no cruise. What was the problem? It was one of his beliefs! He had the crazy belief that it takes money to go on a cruise.

An important element in building big boxes is to stop outlining how the desired goal will manifest. Be open to any and all avenues of possibility. He thought his only option for the cruise was to pay for it with money (a reasonable, but short-sighted view). This man happened to be a good dancer and had even helped teach some dance classes over the years. One day a friend mentioned that cruise lines were always looking for men who were skilled dancers. Cruise lines hire people called "Dance Hosts." These are people who will teach dance lessons and dance with guests in exchange for a free cruise. Guess where I met this man? Teaching dance lessons on his free cruise. As a matter of fact, he had spent the better part of the year dancing his way around the world on a very nice ship.

By outlining that the only way to go on a cruise was with money, he almost stopped himself from achieving his dream. Simply believing that it would cost a lot of money to go on a cruise was a major block for him. Fortunately he kept the dream alive of going on a cruise. This dream, coupled with the new idea of trading some dance lessons, expanded his box big enough that he realized his dream. Our optimistic beliefs are crucial to building big boxes that we love to live in.

Living in a big box is much better than living in a cramped, limited box. The box can be so small it keeps us from meeting new friends or taking an adventure to an exotic land.

The box can be so small that we feel rotten or sick most of the time. Big boxes hold great opulence and prosperity. Successful people have many friends, beautiful homes, fulfilling jobs, and happy families inside their boxes. Small boxes have little room for life's most meaningful experiences. A box can be so big that it includes the sun, the moon, and the stars. Boxes can be so big that you cannot see the walls or the ceiling. You are in charge; make your box any size you desire.

# Chapter 2
# **Components of the Box**

## <u>Ingredients in the Recipe</u>

By using quality conversations, you can configure a life worth living. Nobody creates a wonderful life by complaining and focusing on shortcomings and limitations. If you want to make a really good chocolate cake, use quality ingredients and follow a tasty recipe. Don't use rotten eggs. The same is true in the way you build your life. Don't use rotten thoughts.

Know the components that form big boxes and follow the instruction to build them gigantically. You are the manager in charge of your box. It is up to you to create a wonderful life. Waiting for someone else to do it for you is not only foolish, it is irrational.

It is time to take charge and begin learning the techniques that successful and prosperous people have known for years. Use good ingredients and follow a proven recipe. It is not necessary to reinvent the wheel. There are proven methods and daily practices that empower us to have better lives. Learn about the box you live in and begin to construct it in ways that fit your dreams.

These are the basic components used in building your box:

| | |
|---|---|
| Beliefs | Opinions |
| Feelings | Judgments |
| Perceptions | Thinking |
| Attitudes | Dreams |
| Goals | Habits |
| Interpretations | |

There are behaviors that affect your box:

| Big Box: | Small Box: |
|---|---|
| Helping others | Gossip |
| Positive books/tapes | TV News |
| Dreaming | Finding limitations |
| Teamwork | Complaining |
| Leading | Controlling |
| Love | Resentment |
| Compassion/Understanding | Judgment |
| Willingness | Resistance |

You are the creator of your feelings. You are the creator of your life experience. A primary goal of this book is for you to know and understand that you are always creating something in your life. Every moment of every day, you are creating something by your thoughts and actions.

What are you creating? On the outside you may be creating a house, a job, or a cup of coffee. On the inside you are creating feelings of love or joy, or worry or sadness. The list is endless. How do you create these feelings? With your internal conversations — called thinking or self talk.

## Perceptions and Judgments

Basically, perceptions and judgments are when you see something happen in the world and decide whether it is good or bad. If you decide it is good, you create the feelings of happiness, peace, joy, or love. If you decide it is bad, you create the feelings of sadness, pain, loneliness, anger, or fear. Simply thinking of your past life experiences can bring back those memories. How about the first time you met the love of your life? Or the first time you held your first child? If you take a moment and think back to an occasion like this, can you see what feelings are activated based on your perceptions and judgments?

Take a look at the next example and see if you can find a similar experience in your life. The love of your life walks in the door with two dozen beautiful long stem red roses (court-side seats to a basketball game if you're a man) and you immediately feel joy and excitement. This is because you have a judgment that roses or basketball tickets are a great thing. You don't need time to process the information because your belief system is always "on." So the immediate reaction, based on your split second thinking is 'Oh, this is wonderful.' Not only does your judgment/perception system create the great feeling in the moment, but it can continue to do so for years to come.

On the other hand, let's say that you are seriously allergic to roses and your spouse knows this. What is your reaction? Most likely it will be anger and fear. Without thinking, you will probably flee, angrily yelling at your spouse to get those roses away from you. Next comes the nasty divorce. After the incident, how many times will you tell the story about the "rose incident?" Every time you tell the story feelings that resemble the actual situation, in this case fear and anger, will resurface. These unpleasant feelings will make another appearance yet the roses will be nowhere in sight.

You first make a decision about a situation and then you create a feeling about it. From the previous example, you can see how quickly this happens. You go from seeing, to deciding, to feeling in less than a second based on your beliefs. Change your underlying beliefs and your life will change. Learn to avoid recreating the negative feelings by stopping your detrimental conversations of the story which can get told over and over again. Some people live in the stories they tell over and over about what happened in their past.

The basic components of your box are thoughts and feelings. Your thoughts create the feeling you have. Your feelings are rooted in your thoughts, which are based on your beliefs. This may not be apparent because the feelings come so quickly that you do not notice that you have a thought before the feeling.

Be clear that the thought always comes first. You have an experience, your brain matches it with a belief, and you ask yourself 'is this good or bad?' Then you have YOUR reaction, which is a feeling.

### Chicken or the Million Dollar Egg

Here's an example. A wealthy family member has secretly decided to give you a large sum of money. Without your knowledge, they go to your bank and deposit one million dollars into your account. This wonderful action has taken place but you feel nothing because you know nothing of it. Therefore, you have not made up a belief that it is a good thing. At this point you have a huge amount of money in your account that you know nothing about. Weeks later you get your bank statement and, as usual, you dread opening it. You always see a bank statement as reminding you of how little money you have. You place it on your desk unopened and decide to deal with it later. This is called avoidance and resistance.

Your thoughts about the unopened bank statement create a feeling of dread and anxiety based on your preconceived ideas of it. You are making up a negative story in your mind based on your previous history. You are living in a small box regarding your bank account.

A short note comes in the mail and your relative writes 'I put a little something into your bank account – with Love.'

Finally, you open the envelope and see the deposit and your reaction is excitement and joy. The excitement and joy does not come from the money, but rather from your interpretation that having one million dollars in your account is good. You have a belief that having lots of money is good. This creates good feelings in your body.

The good feelings are not based on the money. Money is simply a number in an account or paper with green ink on it. The joy and excitement is created from the opinion, your opinion, that having one million dollars is a good thing.

Your interpretations, perceptions, and judgments of life experiences, based on your beliefs, create your feelings and reactions. If you want your life to be different, then you must change your beliefs and interpret things in a new way.

## <u>Another Look - at Taxes</u>
Many people have the idea that taxes are bad. The common and obvious belief most people have is that having money is good. People do not like giving money away unless they actually get something tangible in return. Therefore, giving money to the government in the form of taxes is bad, as people do not usually see the tangible return.

In order to champion the belief that taxes are bad, people make up stories to strengthen their position. This could be a story like 'politicians are dishonest and greedy,' 'the government is wasteful,' and 'government workers are lazy and are working just to pick up a paycheck.' The list of stories could go on and on.

People justify these beliefs because it is based on their underlying views and thoughts. With this whole scenario in place, people get a tax bill and then complain, get angry, and resentful. Taxes do not cause anger and resentment, people's <u>interpretation, perception and judgment</u> of taxes do. This is justified through their beliefs and, they get to be right about how wrong the government is through their stories.

If you were to change your belief and interpretation about taxes and the government, you would have other reactions and feelings when the tax bill came. Did you know that you could actually make up a whole new set of beliefs and interpretations, which in turn could create good feelings? The new stories could be told in a more positive light.

A new story could go like this. Your tax money goes to pay for the roads which you love driving your car on. The tax money also goes to pay the teachers who are teaching your children in school. Paying your taxes means that firemen and policemen are ready to come to your aid in case of an emergency. So now you can create a new belief that taxes are wonderful to pay. And, by the way, the more taxes you pay the more money you are making.

Now which belief system is real? Taxes are good or taxes are bad? Taxes are not good or bad; your thinking makes them good or bad. Taxes are just taxes. As Shakespeare enlightened us years ago "There is nothing either good or bad; but thinking makes it so." The belief that taxes are good must be created in your brain and be accepted. Then when you pay your taxes you get to experience a more positive emotion.

So which is true? The one you CHOOSE to believe. The one you CHOOSE to think about. The one you CHOOSE to talk about. It is your choice. The outcomes are clear. The belief that taxes are bad creates resentment and upset in having to pay them. The belief that taxes are worthy creates a sense of goodness for you. The lesson is obvious – create new ways of perceiving things and your life changes.

## Mass Consciousness
The belief that taxes are bad has been created, corroborated, and affirmed by millions of people repeatedly throughout the years. When people join their belief with this huge amount of negativity they create a small box with thick concrete walls reinforced with steel. It is reinforced with the energy of all the other people in the world with the same belief, a type of negative synergy.

Mass consciousness also works for good. When you get enough people thinking something good and the thoughts and energy build and build, eventually the good thing comes into the world. A great example of a mass of people working together to create a big box is the fall of the Berlin Wall. When enough people wanted the wall to come down, they established belief in that possibility and the wall came down.

Can you imagine what would happen if someone could inspire everyone on the planet to believe in a total cure for cancer? If for, say, thirty days, millions and millions of people would believe that we could find a cure for cancer, I firmly believe the cure would be found within a short time. It starts with just one person. Let it be you and when you really believe it, others will be attracted to you and will harmonize with your belief in the cure.

## The Source of Beliefs
Your beliefs are your beliefs. You may have heard someone espouse a belief or opinion but it is up to you to accept it or reject it. Your beliefs are your beliefs because you choose to have them. The only possible exception is children.

When children are young they pretty much accept the beliefs and opinions of the parental figure. Children usually hold their parents as perfect. When a parent asserts a belief, a child has a choice whether or not to place it in his or her own belief system. Children accept and take on their parents' beliefs because there are few choices at a young age. You and I, as adults, have choices in what we accept and reject in regards to our belief system.

It is your duty to search out and eliminate beliefs that are keeping you in small box living situations. Human beings are funny in how strongly they fight for their limiting beliefs. Many of your tired old beliefs no longer serve you, yet you hang on to them because they feel like trusted friends. Maybe you justify this because it is the way you have always thought and you may see no reason to change now. You may even say to yourself, 'This was the way my parents thought and it was good enough for them, so it is good enough for me.' This type of thinking is limiting and must be changed if you want to live life more abundantly.

## Grab the Steering Wheel

Most of the internal chatter you hear in your head comes from authority figures from your childhood: parents, teachers, and older siblings. When you were told something of importance by one of these people and it was said with emotion, it went into your brain in a powerful way. It became embedded and reappears years later as a critical voice.

If you really pay attention, you will actually be able to hear them saying it; especially when you make a mistake. You could call this voice the critical parent voice.

However, it is no longer their voice. It is now yours. You accepted it, probably not consciously in your childhood, but nonetheless, you have it. It is as if they are still criticizing you. They are not. You are. It is your job to be aware that you have stored these thoughts and it is time to throw them out.

When you have a self-critical moment, regardless of what voice you hear, stop for a moment and ask what would be a better way to treat yourself. Would you say this to a small child? No. So tell yourself that you do not have to say it to yourself right now. Know it for what it is. It is just a thought in voice form that can be changed. Begin to change your focus from the critical to the self-compassionate.

People need to get out of the habit of only looking for what is wrong with a person, including themselves, and see what is right. To take it further, we need to stop looking for what is wrong in life situations and begin looking for what is right. Why do people only see their negative attributes when they look in the mirror? Like when a man looks in the mirror and only sees his thinning hair; never seeing his beautiful eyes or fantastic smile. The law is simple, what we focus on expands.

This does not mean that we never see what is wrong, we just need to spend the appropriate amount of time on it and move on to our desires. An easy rule of thumb is 90/10. Spend 10% on what needs to be changed and 90% on what the change is to look like. 10% on what is wrong and 90% on the plan of action to make it right.

Think about the rear view mirror in your car for a moment. The rear view mirror plays an important function in driving your car safely. It shows you what is behind you. What if you only concentrated on the rear view mirror and did not look forward through the windshield? You would not be able to drive very effectively. Many people concentrate only on the rear view mirror in their lives by concentrating on things that happened twenty years ago. They focus on things like how that ex-spouse hurt them or how they did not get the break they needed.

Their conversations are so focused on the past that they rarely look at the present moment or to the future. If they do look at the future, it is based on their negative past that they seem perpetually focused on. If they were driving, it would look like they had their eyes glued to the rear view mirror, rarely looking forward through the windshield. Not only are they focusing on what is behind them, they are trying to steer the car with the rear view mirror. Their hands are firmly clutching the mirror instead of the steering wheel. Not a great way to steer a car, or live a life. Oh, they may occasionally look to what is ahead, but it is warped by the constant attention to what is behind them.

Concentrating on the past perpetuates problems in the now. How can they look to the future while focusing their conversations and attention on the past? Certainly they need to reference the past. Here is where the 90/10 rule applies. They would do well to use the rear view mirror 10% for reference and look forward through the windshield 90% to focus on where they want to go. Nobody gets to where they want to succeed by focusing on where they have been, especially based on their "fender benders."

## Proactive Thinking
Take a moment and think about the following: "You have control over what you think every day." Most likely though, you have not been taught good mental hygiene. It was not

taught in school and unless your parents learned it, they did not teach it either. In school, they taught you how to remember things like multiplication tables and important dates.

This is not active thinking. This is simply reciting, which is a low level of thinking. You must teach yourself to think, really THINK! Active thinking is the goal. If not, you have far too much internal noise and confusion and will be stuck in old thinking behaviors. When a random thought comes into your mind, you are under no obligation to think about it for more than a moment or two. This is especially true with negative thought.

If an angry person knocks on your front door, you do not have to let them in. If you are not proactive in your thinking, you may find the person barging in and staying for dinner. The same is true with our thoughts. They are guests and should be treated accordingly. Be discriminating with the thoughts you host in your mind.

# Chapter 3

# Box Building 101

## Better Conversations

By now you probably have a basic understanding of the actions and components that you have used in building your box. You are also probably somewhat clear about why you want to build a very large box to live in. Mainly, it feels good. Remember, your conversations create your box.

When you build a large box, you live a life that is more productive and more meaningful. Since you are 100% responsible for building the box in which you live, it makes good sense to begin using certain tools that are available to everyone. Understanding and knowing about these tools is not enough, you must use them on a daily basis in order for them to make a difference in your life. Knowing how to make a cup of coffee is not the same as making a cup of coffee. The difference between the two is the action. Utilizing the tools and components is simple but it requires persistence.

Remember, limited beliefs create the boundaries people must live within, or, the walls of the box. Expand your thinking with optimistic possibility thinking and your box automatically expands.

Your only tool in building and maintaining your box is your <u>CONVERSATION</u>. You have only two types of conversations:

1. Conversations with yourself.
2. Conversations with others.

Your conversations are the greatest tool you possess in forming and shaping your box. As a matter of fact, your conversations are the <u>only</u> tool you have to change your life. Conversations are the avenue by which the beliefs you possess manifest in your world.

In essence, you speak and think what you believe to be true. Beliefs come through your conversations. Actions follow belief. Your actions create your life.

Beliefs > Conversations > Actions > Your Life

### Conversations with Self

Take a look at the conversations you have with yourself. Your thinking process is the conversation you are having with yourself. Thinking can be categorized in two ways – intentional thinking, and thoughts that seem to pop in. In the last chapter we looked at the thoughts that just seemed to pop in. Your intentional thinking is the process you get to take control of with concentration and intention.

The conversations you have with yourself are simply the thoughts that you have in your mind. They are stories that are good, bad, and indifferent. Maybe it is going through the grocery list (indifferent). It could be about how much you dislike a situation at work (small box). It may be worry about a financial situation (small box). Or it could be a thought about how much you are looking forward to your upcoming vacation to the beach (big box). All inner dialogue creates something in your state of being. It creates feelings of happiness, confusion, stress, anger or joy, depending on the story. Something like a grocery list probably creates a low feeling level, but a feeling or state of consciousness is always created by your inner conversations.

Again, what about the thoughts that seem to just pop in? We cannot control these, but we can control whether we dwell on them. The question should be: "Does this thought help me feel love, peace, or joy?" If it brings up fear then maybe it should be discarded and another thought consciously chosen that is productive and positive.

## Self Sabotage

Human beings always try to prove that their underlying beliefs are true. It seems people take comfort in knowing the "right" answers. The problem with already knowing the "right" answers is that people stop looking at new ways to solve or improve current problems or situations. If people are convinced that they are "right" about something then they no longer need to look for answers. They are no longer open to any answers.

The human tendency is to hold on to what we believe, even if it is no longer in our best interest. "Being right" probably comes from childhood. It can be traced back to the early school years when you were praised and given good grades for having the right answers to questions, especially on tests. When you had a correct answer, you then imprinted it in your brain and felt a sense of satisfaction in knowing an answer. Human beings find comfort in being right and having the proper answers; hoping for acknowledgment and appreciation for being correct.

## Established Early

Deep-seated beliefs come through in ways that some may find strange. People may have a certain goal that they are working toward, but then find they continually fail over and over again. They take action, which is good, but they have an underlying belief completely opposed to the desired goal.

The underlying belief stopping the person from achieving the goal is called a limiting belief. One such limiting belief might be, 'you have to work hard to make money.' This is a common belief established by parents who did work hard to make a living. This is respectful, but not the only way to make money. We must be open to the many avenues of making money, and yes, some of them are harder than others. However, there are many who do not work hard and make plenty of money. By the way, as an example, I define working hard as picking fruit for 10-12 hours a day in the hot sun. Most of us really do not know hard work.

Another type of limiting belief is one that we put on acceptable behavior. How many times have we heard someone tell their small son "big boys don't cry?" This belief is dragged into adulthood by many men who have shame and embarrassment and cannot bring themselves to show emotion. The self-talk, or internal conversation, tells the men to "hold it together" and "don't let the true feelings show." Not expressing their feelings through tears as adults hinders their relationships with their families and with themselves.

Not crying probably satisfied the parent who wanted the boy to act differently, but it also set up a limiting belief for him. Now, later in life, men find it uncomfortable to show emotion based on the simple belief they accepted and adopted at a very young age. Would you live by the decisions of a five or seven year old? Well, many people are living out the beliefs they adopted when they were mere children. At a young age, they made powerful decisions that are still running their lives.

They may know intellectually that it is okay for a man to cry, but deep down the belief is still there. It is not always easy to adopt a new belief. When a person holds a limiting belief, it seems absolutely real to them, even if they know it is unreasonable. Beliefs are not always reasonable or based on facts. Holding on to limiting beliefs stops many from achieving or getting what they want. Someone may want to get a college degree, but not think they are smart enough so they never even try. They desire to have success with a worthy goal, but deep down do not believe it to be possible. And then action follows belief and they choose to do nothing or an action that does not succeed.

## <u>Same Old Beliefs - Same Old Life</u>
Take a woman who has no money and is holding strong to the belief she must have money to get a new car. A friend begins to explain to her that there may be other possible ways to attain the desired car without money. The woman scoffs at the friend and gets resistant. She begins to tell the friend how unreasonable the idea is. She knows the only way to attain a new car is to have money, and she can prove it. She proves it in her conversation, and then manifests it in the real world by not getting a car due to her lack of money. She gets to be right. Right, but with no money and no car.

People get very attached to their limiting beliefs. Take the mouse who finds cheese at the end of a hallway in a maze. If he finds cheese at the end of the hallway a few times he builds a belief system to that effect. Take away the cheese and the mouse continues to return to the hallway over and over, even though there has been no cheese for many trips.

How many times does the mouse go down the hallway until he learns the cheese is gone? Somewhere in the back of his little mouse brain is the belief he will find cheese there. Repetitious thinking is a way to build beliefs. Or we could say repetitious thinking creates a strong box. In this case the mouse creates a strong small box by persistently doing the same action even though the results are not fruitful.

The box, created by repetitious thinking, can be either a big box or small box, but it will be strong - strong in that it is based on the intensity of the emotions combined with the number and frequency of repetitions. The mouse has a wonderful experience eating the cheese. Getting cheese at the end of a hallway over and over definitely equals a good feeling (intensity) with duplication (repetitions). The mouse could look for other avenues for the cheese and not depend on the one hallway. But most mice do not consider new paths. The mouse has done it this way for years, why change now?

Humans do the same thing. They do the same old behavior, hoping for different results. They do the same old thinking; hoping events will change in their lives. It is time for you and it is time for me to find a new path leading to what we want in life. New thoughts and new thinking is that path.

### Strong Boxes
Big boxes are built with beliefs established in possibility and goodness. Strong boxes are built through repetition. Big strong boxes tend to weather storms and not shrink when challenges arise. Building a big box to live in does not mean that it will not collapse when adversity arises. It is only as strong as the underlying belief you hold.

When someone with a big strong box hits a rough spot, they have the attitude that things will get better, that it always works out. They do not shrink their box and begin to complain and worry. Boxes naturally fluctuate a little during the day. The key is to have the box big and strong so when a failure happens you can take it in stride and stay big.

Some people fluctuate their box wildly during the day. One moment it is big, the next it is small. One moment all is good, and the next life could not be worse. The box goes up and down, up and down. No wonder they are worn out during the day.

Let me give illustrate this. Do you know anyone who is a pessimist? They are always looking at the negative side of life. Obviously they live in a small box. One day they win $10,000 in the lottery. Initially they get excited and their box expands rapidly to be huge. Then they start telling friends things like: 'Well, the IRS wants a huge chunk of it, and my wife wants some for new furniture, and the kids want to go on a trip, there is hardly any left for me. I might as well have never even bought the ticket.' And before you know it, they are back in their small box after winning a nice chunk of money. They are so used to being in the small box they keep creating it that way. The small box they have created is strong and it rebounds right back to the small size they are comfortable with.

Now, reverse that and the exact same thing happens to big box optimists, if they build it strong. Life is good, something bad happens which shrinks their box, but they rebound because they are comfortable in a big box. They know how to take charge and expand their box.

## More Conversations with Yourself
If you want your life to be different, begin having different conversations, especially the ones you have with yourself. You can call these self-talk, affirmations, or just plain thinking. You are an intelligent being that has been given the ability to consciously reason, ponder, and judge. Take control of what you think and stop letting your mind wander to all the negative places it may go.

Let us revisit the reality of how thoughts pop into your mind. Again, you do not have to think anything you do not want to. You cannot stop thoughts from coming in, but you can stop thinking them once you find yourself concentrating in a negative way. Thoughts that pop in may not be supporting your goals. It is up to you to stop thinking them and to consciously choose a thought that sustains and supports your goals. It is a good idea to be ready with a positive thought process to replace any negative thoughts that pop into your mind.

When thoughts come in like 'I am not smart,' 'I can't do this,' 'I hate this,' you immediately have a choice. You may continue to think that thought and all that goes with it. Or, you may take control by saying "Stop," and replace the thought with one that will support you in having what you want.

For example, when a negative thought comes in, say "Stop," and then affirm 'I am smart,' 'I can do this,' or 'I can do this successfully.' Say or think the new thought with feeling and intensity. The negative thought may come back again. And each time, you must say "Stop," and choose another thought, one that is more positive.

It is vital to have backup thoughts, called affirmations, memorized to effectively counter the negative thoughts that come in. Do not expect to stop a thought without replacing it. Your brain must have something to keep it occupied all the time. Just saying stop is not enough. Your brain will go back to the old thought if a new one is not immediately put in its place.

New thoughts equal a new life. It is absurd to believe that anyone can have a new and improved life based on their old thoughts and beliefs. Thinking new thoughts is a powerful way to build a bigger box. Just because the thought comes in does not mean you have to think it. When thoughts pop in, choose whether it is a life-affirming thought or one that needs to be replaced. Invite life-affirming thoughts in and send the negative thoughts on their way.

Be mindful of your thoughts because they are the building blocks to creating a better life for yourself. This is not a new idea, just one that is tried and true.

## Affirmations and Denials
Affirmations are extremely worthwhile to have in your bag of tools. You need every possible tool to rid your mind of negativity. Affirmations are an effective tool in building a big box for yourself. When working on removing negative conversations from your brain, positive inner dialogues are crucial.

You want to have something quick and effective to replace any negative thought you notice. Memorizing affirmations is best, or you can write them on a slip of paper to be pulled out and read at those negative moments. Everyone has these moments when black clouds seem to hang around.

Actually, they are not following you. You are dragging them with you. The clouds represent your choice of negative, self-defeating thinking and the rope you use to drag them around is your continued attention to negative thoughts. Fix your attention on good thoughts and affirmations, and your grip on the rope will release. Those dark clouds will move back into the nothingness from which they came.

Affirmations are easy and simple. They are usually short sentences that clearly state your desires and goals. They need to be in the affirmative, hence the word affirmation. They also need to be in the first person, present tense. So get rid of words like try, will, want, and maybe.

It is easiest to start them off with 'I am…' for example; 'I am healthy and vitally alive, feeling wonderful every moment of this day.' As opposed to 'I want to be healthy and vitally alive, trying to feel wonderful every moment of this day.'

Your affirmations should consist of your goals written on paper in the present tense, as if you have already achieved them. Like, 'I am now making $10,000.00 a month.' Say the affirmations with feeling and intensity. Put a smile on your face and a buzz in your heart. Sing them if you want. The key is to believe them with feeling.

### Conversations with Others
The second types of conversations we have are conversations with other people. This includes verbal and nonverbal communications, written letters, and emails. Basically, this is any form in which you communicate with others. Nonverbal communication includes body language and facial expressions.

Begin to really listen to the conversations you have with others and be prepared to be surprised. People frequently talk without really taking into account what they are saying. People go on automatic pilot in conversing with other people and speak in terms of their limiting beliefs: 'Well, nobody in my family went to college so I knew I wouldn't go,' 'It is going be another scorcher today,' 'I would like to do that, but I am much too shy,' 'Wash the car and it always rains.'

When people talk in such a careless manner, the limited beliefs have a funny way of coming true. People often say these negative statements flippantly or as a joke, but there is a powerful underlying idea at work there. These are thoughts that must be brought into the light of awareness and thrown out to make way for a more positive belief.

This may sound trivial, but these are the conversations that create your life in the moment. These negative conversations are dis-empowering for you and others. If you really want to live powerfully, then have real, authentic conversations about the possibilities in someone's life – especially yours. You don't want to sound boastful in your conversations with others, so speak in ways that are humble, positive, and uplifting in regards to other people.

## Showing People Your Box
You tell people more about who you are within the first three minutes you meet them than you might be aware. Somehow, your underlying beliefs and attitudes come right through in your conversations. When you are communicating with someone they are listening to your words, but more importantly, they are sensing in your tone of voice and facial expressions even more information. With this information, they construct a box in their own mind about who you are as a human being.

Most of us walk around and think nobody really knows who we are. In reality, it is quite the contrary. Who you are, which is your box, is visible right in the middle of your forehead for all to see. You actually tell people your beliefs and attitudes and feelings (your box) all the time. If you have created a small box for yourself, then be very careful. Other people will perceive your small box life and then believe it for you.  Wow, at least two people believing in limitations, your limitations!

After that, every conversation you have with that person will be based on your mutual belief in your limitations.  People build a small box by their limiting, negative conversations and then they enroll others in believing the same limitations with them and for them.  In doing this, you have built a strong, small box to live in.

Let's move this into the positive.  If your conversation is about your grand goals while exhibiting an astounding attitude, they will believe that for you.  That is how they will see your box.  In some way, their conversations will always reflect what they believe about you.  If they think you are wonderful (big box) then they will tell others.  Why not let them help you build your box really big?

Your conversations with others either illustrate the large box that you want to live in, or they portray the small box you are trapped in.  You trap yourself in small boxes by having conversations of lack, pity, victimhood, anger, resentment, the list goes on.  Unless the other person is really awake and committed to his or her own personal transformation, they will accept your limiting conversations as true and then be unconsciously supporting your failure.  These may be people who love you, but are not yet awake to the power of conversations in creating successful lives.

## Where Do Feelings Come From?
Words of anger with another person can create animosity in the moment.  Conversations are a creative process and words make up conversations.  Words of judgment create

the feelings of being unwanted in the moment. Words of limitation create a sense of futility and powerlessness. Conversations generate feelings. There is one rule if you want to feel good in life. You must be committed to changing the majority of your conversations to ones that are supportive of good feelings.

We all know people who have been telling a story about someone who wronged them 10 years ago. They have told the story so many times that they have it polished like a shiny, prized marble. Every time they tell the story they get right into the drama as if it happened yesterday. They recreate the feelings of anger or victimhood once again simply by retelling the story. This creates negative feelings squeezing the box smaller and smaller. Conversations are a creative process creating feelings and emotions.

Why not tell a story about something that happened years ago that puts love in your heart. Maybe the first time you met your spouse or when you landed that big client. These stories create something positive in you. Stories are powerful tools in changing your life for the better. Listen to the stories people tell on a daily basis. Choose someone that you know who is always negative and see if you can find a pattern in his or her conversations. Then do the same with someone who is successful and happy. The person who is successful and happy will tell stories that are uplifting and optimistic. They have found the power in creating big boxes out of positive conversations.

## The 100% Game
There is a wonderful game that participants in my workshops love to play. It is called "The 100% Game." The process includes telling your partner about what your life is like as if it is already 100% successful. You get four

minutes to tell your partner, in vivid detail, what it is like to have great health, a happy loving family, lots of money, and success in business.

First, determine what your goals are in your life. Then, talk to your partner as if the goals were already achieved. In the game, each participant must tell their goals as if they have already come true regardless of any current circumstances. One man in a wheelchair since birth passionately spoke of actually running in a 10k race to raise money for a favorite charity. A woman talked of wearing a size six dress and having heads turn as she walked into a party. Yet another talked of anonymously donating money to build a new addition for her church with an expanded Sunday school for children.

Each of these stories inspired and uplifted them while sharing with their partner. The 100% game always raises the energy in the room. I ask why they feel so good, and they say things like: 'Because we are talking about our dreams,' 'Because it is all positive,' 'It felt like it was real,' and 'I could see that I could really do it.'

Actually, the only thing that was real was a conversation between two people. Everything else was an idea about the future, which has not come true yet. Since one of the fundamental teachings of this book is that every conversation creates something, then what got created? Emotions, feelings, and energy were generated. The people feel alive during this process, excited with hope. Not only do they get excited by talking about their own goals; they get excited about hearing their partner's goals.

What would happen if I asked them to take four minutes and talk to their partners about all their current problems and limitations? Where do you think the energy of the participants would go? The emotion in the room would feel heavy and depressed.

What is the biggest lesson in this exercise? Conversations are powerful tools used to create feelings in the present moment. Maybe it can be more clearly stated in this way: "When I think about and talk about my dreams and goals, I feel great."

It is also a lot of fun listening to your partner for four minutes talking about their incredible life. You get to watch and listen as your partner gets enthusiastic about living the life they have dreamed of. Not only are you being supportive, but you actually want to help your partner achieve their goals. People love being supportive and encouraging. This is one of the big joys in life: being on a team and helping one another achieve their life goals.

The next big lesson in the exercise is that when one person is supportive of the other person they feel empowered. The teaching here is: "When I support and encourage another person's success, I feel great." Of all the motivational and success wisdom taught over the years, this is the most important lesson. If you want to be successful in life, the easiest way to do that is to help other people achieve success. Zig Ziglar's teaching is "If you help enough people get what they want, you will get what you want."

## Your Current Box Size
Why all this talk about boxes when the book is supposed to be about conversations? Because you live in a box and its size is determined by your conversation. How do you know how big your box is? The easiest way to determine your box size is to check how you feel. Look at the results in

your life. Notice what your predominate thought process is. If you are not getting the results you want in your life, you need to check out your thinking and your actions. Actions always reflect what a person really thinks and believes.

If a person's underlying belief is that they cannot achieve something, then their actions will reflect it in ways that seem reasonable and justifiable. They will unconsciously block their own success. They may create a story about how they really did not want it anyway. Or they may say they do not really deserve it. They may even believe that someone or something is keeping it from them. This is called victimhood.

These excuses and justifications will all sound plausible and reasonable. However, the excuses are in support of the underlying limiting belief in non-achievement or failure. It takes conscious effort on your part to diligently look at your thought process. Your thoughts, conscious and unconscious, are creative all the time.

Take time each day to ask yourself if your thinking and actions are supportive of what you say you want. Be careful not to accept limiting ideas from other people. Just because someone thinks a certain way about you does not mean that it is so.

It is like a baseball. Someone may throw a baseball, or limited idea, at you. You then make a choice to catch the ball and play with it, or you can look at it and let it pass by. If you don't like the idea someone throws your way, then don't catch it and certainly don't hold on to it. Let it fly by and then remind yourself of the truth. You are a wonderful person capable of achieving great success. Let the negative thought from the other person disappear or roll off like water off a duck's back.

Just because someone thinks you are stupid does not make you stupid... unless you accept the belief. When people throw small boxes at you, do not accept them. As a matter of fact, dodge them and let them pass you by, unscathed. For some reason, people love to throw small boxes at others. Small boxes are limiting or negative ideas like: 'The economy is so bad companies are not hiring,' 'You are a nice person, but do not have what it takes to succeed in sales,' 'You never have been able to lose weight.' The list could go on for pages.

You can listen, but it does not mean you have to accept other people's opinions. You are intelligent. Act intelligently by listening to what others have to say. Judge if it is worthy or not worthy, and take appropriate action. Be open to criticism as a tool that can help you become a better person. It may be uncomfortable listening to it, but there may be some truth in it. Even if the person says the thing in an attacking way, listen for any information that may help you act more successfully.

And if small boxes are thrown your way, do not grab them. The box says more about the person throwing it than it does about the person it is thrown at.

## Avoiding Small Boxes
When you hold a small box for someone else, you must hold and experience it first. So if you judge someone as greedy or stupid, then you hold that idea in your brain and you get to react and have the feelings of judgment and righteousness first. In essence, if you hold small boxes about other people, you live in them first. Judgment, condemnation, and

resentment are truly small negative boxes that trap people and keep them from experiencing life to the fullest. Throwing a small box at someone else has the effect of a boomerang.

Be careful in telling other people that they have a small box. You may think you are being helpful, which may be the case, but it can also be a disguised jab or put down. It could be done with an air of righteousness and superiority. In that case, telling the other person they have a small box in reality only shrinks your box. Thoughts and judgments held in your mind affect you first. If they ask for feedback on themselves or their behavior, then you can sincerely help them out.

Only give feedback and opinions when asked and be mindful in doing it. Telling someone they are flawed without permission does not help them and it does not extend the hand of compassion. If someone asks for help or guidance, then you can support them in ways they can feel empowered and useful. Encouraging others is a sure way to expand your own box. If done sincerely, others can be empowered more effectively build a bigger box for themselves. Encouraging and uplifting another person always builds a bigger, stronger box for you.

## Your Choice

Many people are not willing to look at their beliefs and to change the size of their box. Why? Because they think the box only comes in one size and it takes too much effort to change. By reading this book, you, on the other hand, have made a choice to look at yourself and begin the process of self-evaluation. By just picking up this book you have expanded your box. Your box can only stay expanded as long as you continue to think in new and uplifting ways. I love the adage, "Your brain is like a parachute; it works best when it is open."

**Below is a list of Box shrinking behaviors:**
1. Choosing to believe limiting beliefs from childhood.
2. Not consciously thinking about the content of your conversations during the day.
3. Repeating the same old negative conversations which create the same old negative results.
4. Condemning others by what they look like, how they act, and believing the negative things others might say about them.
5. Choosing to let negative feelings and worry dictate your actions and thinking.
6. Freely accepting small boxes thrown by other people.
7. Not taking responsibility for your current box. If your box is small it is because you created it that way.
8. Having your conversations filled with complaints.
9. Having conversations focusing on how bad things are and focusing on limitations.
10. Worry filled thinking.

To have a different life, you must change your conversations. Changing your conversations builds bigger boxes. I realized I was complaining too much. Most of my conversations were about what was wrong and who was wrong. People that I liked were not spending much time with me anymore. Then I looked at the people I had attracted into my life and they were negative individuals. It was a tough lesson, but I realized I was attracting people just like myself.

I decided to be vigilant about my conversations and to stop complaining. One day the decision was made to stop all of my complaining – cold turkey. I caught myself on numerous occasions about to speak, and realized that complaining was about to come forth in my conversation. So I would simply stop talking. I came to the conclusion, a scary one, that I really did not have a whole lot to talk about. As I continued with my commitment of no complaining, it became easier, but the temptation of the habit stayed around for months. Over time, I taught myself new ways of conversing with everyone in my life and I was able to have more positive conversations.

## Stay Awake

Consciously listening to yourself on a daily basis requires persistence and a true desire to change. There must be the self-motivation of wanting to make your life better. Listening to your conversations can be challenging. Human beings, for the most part, do not like challenges, and will avoid change. As a matter of fact, some of the greatest stresses we face in life are changes like moving to another city, getting a new job, getting married or having children.

Can you make change fun and exciting? Yes, if you have a clear focus and passionate goals to keep you motivated. You may find yourself in the middle of a change feeling stressed or unhappy. You will then need something positive to focus on. It may also be the necessity to change some underlying negative beliefs about the situation. You could create a new story based on your goals with a new perspective and be willing to believe it is already true. It will be a big leap, a necessary leap. A problem cannot be solved at the level of the problem. The problem will best be solved by focusing on the desired outcome. Make sure the new idea is something you passionately desire.

# Chapter 4
# Building Bigger Stronger Boxes

## Thoughts and Feelings, Your Choice

By now you understand that you are always building the box you live in, whether you like it or not, or even whether you are aware of it or not. You are constantly having conversations with yourself and other people which means you are always building your box. You are now ready to begin the process of expanding your box. Your job is to become a *Master Box Builder*. Remember the walls of the box are elastic and you may expand them or shrink them based on whether the conversation is positive or negative.

As an example, you may have a day at work filled with success and accomplishment. You leave work feeling strong and positive. Your box is really big and you feel terrific. After getting in your car, you find yourself in a traffic jam that is keeping you from getting to an important engagement. Consciously or unconsciously, you decide that being stuck in traffic is a bad thing because it is keeping you from being at this dinner party. Restlessness, agitation, anger, frustration – these are the normal feelings that arise for most people. Are these emotions serving you in the current situation? Probably not.

Feelings of restlessness, agitation and anger arise based on your belief that you should be someplace other than in traffic. This is simply a belief you hold in your mind. It is not unreasonable to want to be at a dinner party with friends rather than stuck in traffic. However, this belief is creating a state of frustration and anger. A choice must be made. Keep the reasonable belief and be frustrated, or adopt a new belief and experience peace in the midst of traffic. Easier taught than done. But it can be done. A new belief must be created in the box. A belief like, 'Traffic is a great time to be quiet and do some positive thinking,' or 'I can be a bit late and make a grand entrance.' You get the idea. Change the belief and your feelings change, or stay with the reasonable belief and the feelings stay uncomfortable. This is how you create your moment to moment experiences of living in your box.

## Establishing Strong Beliefs
Establishing a strong belief system, or building a big strong box, is based on intensity of thought, repetition, and confident conviction. Big boxes are built one thought at a time like a brick wall. The wall is built one brick at a time with the bricks supporting one another and weaving themselves into a pattern of strength. The key is to keep your thoughts and feelings focused on what you want – your goals. Later in the book you will have the opportunity to write out your goals. Having them written clarifies them.

To build big boxes you must not focus on the outer circumstances of life with too much attention. Outer circumstances are only one part of the process. Focusing on a low bank balance makes the process of making money that much harder. You may need to know about the low bank account, but do not focus on it. Focus on what you want, not on what you don't want.

If you let outer circumstances dictate how you are living, then you are letting outer circumstances build your box for you. Obviously, this is not an effective or desirable way to live. As stated above, while it is prudent to take stock of a situation, it is not wise to focus your energy and actions solely there. We live in a world much bigger than what we can see.

People who shoot at targets do not focus on the gun or the bullets. They focus on the target, especially the place on the target they want to hit. The gun and the bullets are simply the tools they use to hit the target. Big box builders expand their box by visualizing hitting the bull's eye before they pull the trigger.

Olympic divers do the same thing. While standing on the diving board high above the water, they see themselves making the perfect dive. They hear the crowd cheering and feel what it is like to dive and enter the water perfectly. They see themselves standing on the winner's platform, receiving the gold medal, feeling elated and proud. Then they make the dive.

## Sixteen Seconds for LIFE

Do you understand how your beliefs, feelings, and actions build the box you choose to live in? No doubt you are motivated to change your life if you are this far into reading this book. You are ready to learn the *Sixteen Seconds for LIFE* exercise. It is a very simple activity in building a bigger box for yourself. You may use this to achieve a goal or just to create a good feeling for yourself in a chosen situation. Either way you are creating something good for yourself, namely a bigger box.

When you need to expand your box, take a moment to get present and think about something good in your life for sixteen seconds. Look at something in the real world, or create a picture in your mind. Interpret it as good and think about all the virtuous aspects it possesses. Allow yourself to connect to the feeling that is generated. Experience it as authentic and genuinely real for the whole sixteen seconds.

L Look
I Interpret
F Feel
E Experience

## Step 1 - **Look**

You are looking for a clear idea to focus on. It could be a goal you desire, a feeling you prefer in this moment, or a positive outcome in an upcoming situation. The key here is to get a clear picture in your mind or with your eyes. If you need a quick feeling of peace in a stressful situation then look out the window at some flowers or a beautiful home. You could even get a picture out of a magazine. Anything will work as long as you can see it in your mind or in your world. Make sure it is something that is pleasing to you.

## Step 2 – **Interpret**

Once you have a clear picture, interpret the picture as good, wonderful, beautiful, peaceful, uplifting, and/or radiant. With your mind, think of all that is good about it. Find what is exceptional and praiseworthy in it. Your interpretation is going to lead you to a feeling, so make the interpretation strong and persuasive.

## Step 3 – **Feel**

With a clear picture and an uplifting interpretation, you will begin to feel something good. This is where you want the whole process to take you. You want to feel good. Everyone wants to feel good. And in sixteen seconds you can do that for yourself. Bask in the feeling. Smile. Feel the warmth. Let the feeling lift you. Let it restore your body to a state of health and relaxation. Feel. Feel. Feel.

## Step 4 – **Experience**

Now let yourself, especially your body, experience what you have just given it – a gift that cannot be bought. You have just infused your body with a powerful, cleansing energy. Feelings are energy and they can uplift if they are positive, but they can also bring on stress if they are negative. This is an experience of sixteen seconds. Give it to yourself.

Clear ideas and good feelings are the components of strong big boxes. Practice LIFE several times a day. People who have been stressed for years may <u>need</u> numerous sessions every hour. People who have been living in big boxes for years will also <u>want</u> to perform several sessions every hour. If people wonder what you are doing, tell them. Teach them this simple process. Maybe it will touch their lives as it has touched countless others.

## <u>There is More to Life than Driving a Mercedes</u>

Having good ideas, clear goals, and focused attention are the main ingredients in goal setting. Allow your focus to include more than a bigger house and a more expensive car. There is more to life than achieving material goals. While there is great joy in achieving a goal and having nice things, it can be short-lived. How about creating joy in the process of achieving your goals? Expand your life experience by enlarging your focus to include your values and purpose in life. Certainly, you can have goals that include cars, and watches, and houses, etc. While these are wonderful to own, they will not bring happiness. Happiness can only come from a life lived from your values.

If your happiness is based on your home there could be a problem. A house is nice and brings great comfort, but if it gets blown away by a storm, so could the happiness. Nobody wants to lose a house, but there is more to life than a house.  People find that when they are clearly living from their values, they are most happy.  When their values are illustrated in their life, it matters not if they have huge amounts of money.  Happiness does not come from money.  It comes from a person's values and beliefs.  People who say they will be happy once they get money will probably not be happy, even if money comes.

What brings happiness and joy to people?  Friends, family, a relationship with God, being able to contribute positively to society, leaving the world a little better than the way they found it.  Very basic, but how true.  Having money and nice cars is great, but they are of the physical world and will not last eternally.  Love will last eternally.  It is our job to build our box with a foundation of love.  A great way to do this is to bring your heart into your box.

### TV is Great, Right?
Many talk shows try to outdo each other with appalling guests talking about repulsive things.  They verbally assault each other and sometimes the assaults turn violent with people getting physically hurt.  It is trashy TV.  Even though it is trashy, the ratings are good and good ratings bring in money.

Oprah, at one time, joined the pack of wolves by bringing to her show some pretty trashy topics and guests.  She did this in response to competition and her ratings soared.  For a few years, she lowered the quality of guests for ratings.  Ratings went up, money went up, but her inner fulfillment as a powerful person went down.  Since she owns the show, she decided to make a change.  It became clear to her that through her popularity she affected many people's lives – millions of people watched her show every day.  No doubt this weighed heavily on her conscience.

She took a stand and told the world she would no longer perpetuate such negativity on TV. She did this in the face of potential low ratings and the possibility of losing her show and her popularity. This no doubt was a difficult decision to make, with the consequences possibly affecting her livelihood. In the face of uncertainty, she made the decision to create a show that would empower and uplift people. I can just imagine the network people trying to convince her not to change the format because it was working, i.e., bringing in money.

She said no, and changed the format to bring in topics such as good health, spirituality, inner growth, and helping people. Oh, she probably lost some of her audience who were more interested in negativity. Did her show fall in ratings with the new format? No. As a matter of fact, she is still at the top and look at the difference she is making for people around the world. Like her or not, she is living from her values and continues to live life to the fullest.

She inspires thousands of people every year to help raise money for numerous charities. One year it was collecting spare change for an endowed scholarship for college tuition. People all over the country came in droves to bring buckets of their spare change for her college charity. Now the endowments are sending many students to college who may not have been able to go. She has built a huge box – a global box. She loves inspiring people to not only change and work on themselves, but to also give back to their communities.

What inspires me most about her and her big box building capabilities is that she is so wealthy she would never have to work another day in her life if that is what she chose. Yet she works just as diligently today as she did in the early years. She works because she believes working is good and it enables her to touch millions of lives positively. She did not quit when people threw small boxes at her in the early days. She did not quit when they warned her nobody wanted to listen about positive living. They said she did not "look good" in an afro and that she was overweight. She was so clear about who she was and what she wanted that all those small boxes bounced off with no effect. She persevered and kept in her own mind an expanded box of possibilities and dreams. Oh, she may have grabbed one or two of the small boxes and felt hurt or angry, but *Master Box Builders* like Oprah don't hold small boxes very long. They stay focused on the big box goals, even in the face of opposition, and live life brilliantly with an awesome sense of radiance.

## <u>Prayer Creates Big Boxes</u>
People pray to God for many things such as, money, a good job, or good health. These are worthy things to pray for. God wants good for each and every one of his children. So why don't the prayers get answered? Is God up in Heaven with a list of all the prayers saying yes to some and no to others? I find that hard to believe. Most likely, prayers are not answered because we are not aligning our actions with the prayers. Rev. Eric Butterworth has taught for many years: "God can do for us only that which He can do through us." When we pray we need to move our feet.

People will pray for something like money, and then sit at home in front of the TV waiting for God to answer their prayer. Similar to waiting for the pizza delivery guy. Every few hours they may get up off the couch and run to their front door expecting God to make the money delivery. When it is not there, they go back to watching TV again. A little later, they go back to look on their doorstep and see that no money has arrived. Of course, they have done little personal action in taking responsibility for having the prayer answered. Should God do it all? I think not.

If the money does not come, the person makes up a story that God does not want them to have it or it is not in God's timing. It would be great if we could pray and then poof, God would deliver. But God already delivered, God gave us intelligence, strength, wisdom, and energy. It would be wise for us to use them in conjunction with prayer and action. God can provide money in an infinite amount of ways and we are to do our part of the work. Why do we think God is going to do it for us when there are so many opportunities awaiting us? Maybe, instead of praying for money we ought to pray for financial opportunities and the energy to act on them.

While God can certainly perform miracle healings, great wisdom was given to doctors. If you pray for healing, be open to all the different avenues God might use to heal you. People get so focused on the way they want their prayers answered, they pass right by their good without recognizing it. If a person who is sick tells a story of only wanting to take natural remedies like herbs, are they not limiting God's ability to heal them? While herbs may be a natural and worthy route, it may not be the path for the healing that is being prayed for. Pray. Don't limit God's avenues for the prayer, and take intelligent action that is in alignment with the prayer. Pray and then take the next intelligent activity.

I have friends who use magnets to take away their aches and discomforts. From these magnets, they have attained vitality, energy and health. Magnets would not be on the top of my list for a hurting back. As a matter of fact, I hurt my back and would not even touch the magnets offered. It seemed too, well, too new age "woo woo." This was a small box belief on my part that surely limited my healing. After doctors and medication helped little, I became willing to try anything. Guess what? Those silly little magnets I laughed about brought me back to health. My limited, small box thinking almost kept me from one of God's healing avenues.

### Fly with the Eagles
When opposition or failure presents itself in your life you have a choice to make. You can quit and accept defeat, or you can recommit to your vision and goal, and take another action that is in alignment with your goal. Choosing to quit is building a small box. Complaining about opposition or failure is building a small box. Building a large box may require the enrollment of support from fellow workers, friends or family. You may need encouragement and assistance in holding to your vision.

Big box builders usually have a strong team behind them. If your team is in the workplace, then it is part of your job and theirs to hold to the vision of possibility and success for the company. This creates the environment for an expanded box. If you are working alone, sit with a couple of trusted friends or co-workers, explain your goals, and ask them to support you by only speaking positively about the goals. Positive encouraging words ought to be the tone of all discussions. Every conversation you have with yourself and or others creates a box that you live in. Avoid potential small box building communications that include complaining, limitations, and pessimism.

There will be a problem if the people you share your goals with cannot see the possibility of your success. Even a little doubt can affect their box, which in turn can affect your box. When their doubting creates a small box for themselves, how does it affect your box? Every conversation they have with you will be based on their disbelief. Why? Because, if they do not believe, it can tarnish and color their conversations with you. They may want to believe in your success very much, but people always illustrate in their conversations what they truly believe. It may be very subtle or it may be very clear. They may feel guilty for not believing and then cover up their disbelief by saying positive things. Rest assured that their disbelief will surface in their tone of voice, choice of words, and certainly their actions in regards to your goals.

## He looks SOOOO Big

In one of my seminars, five volunteers come to the front of the room and I have four people lift the biggest one of the five straight up out of a chair using just their fingertips. Four of them circle around the person in the chair and I ask them to position their fingers under the person's arms and knees and to lift. They struggle and strain and usually don't even budge the person. This is because they are not working as a team.

After the failure, I look in each person's eyes and ask them if they believe they will be able to lift the person if we try again as a team. Some have seen the exercise before and know they will be able to lift the person out of the chair. Others will smile and say yes, but inside have disbelief. Their disbelief comes from focusing on the outer appearances, like how big the person is. We fail in life when we make decisions based solely on outer circumstances. Successful people build their belief systems based on desired outcomes not on current facts.

If just one person in the group has disbelief, it affects the whole lifting process. One of two things happens when someone in the group disbelieves. The group either fails to lift the person or they struggle with great effort in the process. This is easily shifted to success if the group is stopped and the people who doubt are convinced in a belief of possibility. What this takes is my confidence in the process. I look them in the eye and tell them that I do this every week and that every week we lift the person out of the chair. Again, with conviction and confidence, I tell them I have seen people bigger than the one in this chair be lifted straight up, as if they were light as a feather, when the group works as a team.

With my long history of lifting people out of a chair, I convince them they will do it this time and it will be ten times easier. Then I ask them if they think I believe they can do it. I am very convincing because I have done this so many times. Inevitably they all agree that I believe, but one or two will still have some doubt. Then I ask the critical question. "Can you believe in my belief?" In order for there to be success in the lifting exercise, I must get them to some type of belief. If they can believe in my belief, then they have enlarged their box enough for possibility to be established. We have NEVER failed.

I build a very big box for them to believe in. Clarity of vision supported with confidence is the key for the successful leadership of a team. Once the team members have a clear vision, confidence, and a combined belief, the person is easily lifted out of the chair as if they were light as a feather. The person who had the disbelief is always shocked at how easy it turned out to be.

Most of the participants say that the basic teaching of the exercise is teamwork. I agree teamwork is an important element. However, having done this exercise for years has taught me that no matter how strong the people, if just one person does not believe then it hinders the success. Belief is crucial to this process and the leader must set the tone. Coaches and leaders must passionately set the goal and vision for the team's victory, and convey it in a convincing way.

## Building Big Boxes with Leadership
Big box builders are leaders. They inspire confidence and compassionately lead others in the same method they would want to be led. Successful leadership hinges on two simple factors.

Have a clear and worthy vision.
Articulate it so that it inspires enthusiasm in others.

My definition of leadership is:
**Leadership is the clear communication of a worthy goal that inspires action.**

When you decide to create success in your life, you will understand the need to become a leader in your life. Nobody drifts his or her way to the top of the mountain. It is your role to be the leader and visionary for your goals. Don't wait for others to lead you; they may or may not lead you to where you really want to go.

Your job is to be clear about what you want in life – your goals. Once you are clear and have committed yourself to the goals, then you can enroll other people into your dream. For instance, if you are building a business, then practice speaking about your business in a positive uplifting way. When people ask what you do, you want to be able, in one or two clearly stated sentences, to impart the core essence of your business with confidence and enthusiasm. If you ramble on and on unfocused, they will most likely leave the conversation confused and uninspired.

Practice the sentence so you intelligently and enthusiastically paint a picture they would be interested in. Do not try to tell them everything in one sitting, as this will overwhelm them. Tell them briefly about your vision in such a way that invites them to ask questions. When they ask questions, it will give you the opportunity to fill in more of the picture. Remember that you want them on your side and very possibly a part of your vision or business. Either way, you want them thinking and speaking positively about you and your goals. Let them help you in creating a big box.

## Rampage of Appreciation

Appreciation is the one tool that you can utilize in building a big box quickly and effectively. Do not underestimate the power of appreciation. Everyone, including you and me, wants to feel good. The only way to feel good is to create it within yourself by applying your thinking abilities. Your thoughts create feelings and change the way you feel all day long. Change your thoughts, and your feelings and your emotional life will change.

Perception and judgment are part of the everyday group of brain functions you have. When you perceive something as bad and then judge it, your body creates a corresponding feeling. Your perception and judgment can be conscious or unconscious. When people do not take conscious control of their thinking they run into trouble. For instance, is the glass half full or half empty? The answer creates a feeling and thought process that either supports a good feeling or just the opposite. Remember, all thought, including perceptions and opinions, create a box. When you see the glass half full, you are creating a big box by looking for what is right and what is positive. Seeing the glass half-empty focuses on lack and insufficiency which of course leads to a small box.

Your task is to find situations and things you can appreciate which will then give you a good feeling. Search, quest, probe, rummage, hunt, scour, explore, seek, pursue, hound, stalk, chase for positive situations and things you can love and appreciate. The purpose of the rampage of appreciation is to feel good which leads to your experiencing a bigger box. A great way of doing this is to begin to see good everywhere you look. Instead of seeing traffic, look for the beauty in the trees by the side of the highway. Look for snazzy cars that you can admire and fantasize about. Traffic does not have to be a horrible experience. As a matter of fact, there is nothing good or bad about traffic; a person's attitude and judgment create it one way or another. Choose to connect your thoughts on the positive. There is always something good in every situation. Focus on that good, and your feeling experience in that moment will benefit you.

Going on a rampage of appreciation can be quite fun and create outrageous good feelings. What better way to live in your huge box than to have outrageous good feelings? People will begin to be attracted to you and want to work and play with you. Pessimists do not like to spend time with optimists. They will be repelled while other optimists will want to have you as a friend and colleague.

Where and what can you appreciate? Open your eyes and everything you see is fair game. Look around your house and look for what you love about it, the windows, the pictures on the wall, and the color of the paint. The list can go on and on. Take a moment and do your *Sixteen Seconds for LIFE.* The goal here is to expand your box by upgrading your thinking and feeling.

## Rampage of Appreciation for Yourself

Building a big box requires a healthy sense of self. Forget being egotistical and self centered. This is about looking for the good in yourself and appreciating it. Self-worth is built on your beliefs and attitudes about who you are. In the "Twenty-One Days to Becoming a Master Box Builder" in the last chapter of this book, you are instructed to look for the good in yourself for one full day.

Look into the mirror and instead of looking at the wrinkles or gray hair, look at what you like about yourself. Look for what people have complimented you on. Just take a moment and look and appreciate yourself. Smile. Take a breath in. Relax. Accept yourself in that moment as a wonderful person. This may sound sort of hokey, but in reality it feels good and is effective in building your box to huge proportions.

Throughout the day, look for activities that you are doing and give yourself credit for them. Give thanks for the values in which you live your life. Acknowledge yourself for the way you treat people. Every time you think about your box, give yourself a boost and hunt for a quality or feature about yourself that you can lavish on yourself for sixteen seconds.

## Rampage of Appreciation for Others

It is a commonly known fact that people love to be sincerely appreciated and acknowledged. The key word here is sincerely. When interacting with people in your family, or work, or at the grocery store, look for something you can appreciate about them. Maybe the way they are dressed or a piece of jewelry or even their hair. Don't go on and on about it, make a simple sincere remark.

Don't limit the appreciation to just the way they look. Acknowledge their actions, the way they handled a project or even the attitude they project in life. There are so many things to appreciate about others as long as you are looking and are dedicated to expanding your box. People love to be around others who like them. One of life's treasures is having deep friendships and the ability to affect people's lives in a positive manner. Appreciate them and learn effective ways to encourage them.

## Chapter 5
# Empowering Others to Build Bigger Boxes

### Affecting Other People's Boxes

You are 100% responsible for building your own box, and other people are 100% responsible for building theirs. We do not have the power to expand or contract other people's boxes. We cannot feel their feelings, or think their thoughts, or form their attitudes which are the basic components of box building. People must take responsibility for building their own box and we must let them. If a person is feeling badly, we must understand they created it. And if a person is feeling good, we must know they created that. It could be in response to something we did or said, but their feelings are created within them.

People love to think that others can give them love. Nobody can give another person love. Love is not a tangible thing a person can hold and give to another. Someone can do something kind and thoughtful, and then the other person can interpret this as good, which leads to the feeling. The feeling comes not from the action of the other, but from the interpretation of the action. Feeling loved is a feeling we generate ourselves.

Even though everyone creates their own feelings, we do influence people through our conversations and actions. If I say something malicious to someone, I know they will probably perceive it in a negative light and create a feeling of hurt or anger. They do not have to interpret it this way, but most people would. In conversing with others, it is my responsibility to be aware of the words I choose and the tone in which I convey it. We do influence people by our conversations and actions.

This influence is based on our relationship with them. Parents have powerful influence over their children. Teachers have influence over their students. A spouse also has influence over his or her mate. You often have influence in people's lives because they trust you or look up to you. Think about this for a moment. Someone can tell you that your hair is a bit out of sorts. But if your spouse says this, it may take on a whole new meaning. It could be perceived as a judgment with negative effects. It could also be perceived as a loving act that only someone you trust would be safe in sharing with you. Again, it is your perception and judgment that leads to your reaction and feelings.

Our conversations with others can be compared to boxes; boxes that we put in front of others. When I speak positively to someone, it is as if I am holding up a really big box in front of him or her. They then look at the large box I am projecting and, hopefully, accept it. If I tell someone they are beautiful, I am holding this big box called "You are beautiful." The person hears it, looks at it, and then decides to accept it or not. If they accept it, they then take the box and adopt this belief as their own, which increases the size of their box.

The same would be true of a negative opinion like "You are stupid." It would be as if I threw this small box called "stupid" at them. As the box flies toward them, they must make a choice. Grab it and believe it, or let it go by untouched. If they grab it, their box immediately shrinks and they believe they are stupid. However, if they see the small "stupid" box coming their way, they can look to their belief system, see if it matches or is in conflict, and not accept the box. Hence their box is unaffected.

Small boxes get thrown around all the time. People who are moving through life half-awake tend to pick up small boxes without thinking. Then they wonder why they feel bad. They feel bad because they are accepting negative beliefs from other people. When a small box gets thrown your way, take a moment and dodge it, deny it, let it pass. Just because someone throws a small box at you does not mean you have to adopt it. Just because someone says you are stupid does not mean you are, or that you need to believe it.

Turn yourself into a large box manufacturer. Look for ways to show people large boxes about themselves when you are conversing with them. Talking about gossip, problems, or blame will shrink both your boxes. If you doubt this, the next time you are focusing a conversation on problems, check to see how each of you feel. You will certainly find yourselves feeling a low energy level and have some type of negative feeling.

## Empower People
Inspiring others to build big boxes is one of life's most rewarding and powerful feelings. We do this with children when we teach them to read or play soccer. We do this when we encourage someone to take a risk and achieve something they thought was impossible. We do this when we simply get present with another human being and love and accept them for who they are in that moment.

Traveling on a weekly basis allows me to meet many people from all walks of life. One of my favorite questions when I meet someone is, "If your life could be any way at all, how would you like it to be?" Then I stop and focus my attention and listen. They are usually taken aback because this is not a question usually asked. People are accustomed to simple conversations that don't create very much. Conversations like news, weather, and sports.

By asking what they really want in their lives, I give them the opportunity to speak and get clear about their forgotten dreams and goals. This conversation usually lightens them up and adds a sparkle in their eye. They smile as they talk. It is sad that only 5% of our population have their goals written down on paper. People may want their lives to be better, but if they don't write their goals down they will most likely never achieve them. I love motivating people to look within themselves and define their goals.

What are they actually doing? They are expanding their box in the moment with their conversation. They are talking about their goals, passions, and dreams. They are also clarifying and cultivating their life's purpose. They are talking about goals becoming reality. They are taking a moment to dream again. Seeing what is possible brings them into a feeling state of joy. The interesting part of this activity is they always talk about things that are really possible.

All the goodness in your life starts with a good idea that you believe in. That is the power of conversations. Conversations create and build boxes and we are always having conversations with ourselves or with other people. The conversations you have with people can be plain and create very little, they can be detrimental and damaging, or they can be empowering and uplifting. Learning and polishing your skills in conversation can uplift yourself and others to a new way of living successfully with great joy and fulfillment.

## Set an Example

Building a bigger, expanded box for yourself is an example to others that it can be done. If you listen to entrepreneurs who have been successful, they all end up saying the same thing: "If I can do it, anyone can." Yes, they probably worked hard and had a clear purpose and vision, but it is also true that anyone can do what they did if someone wants it badly enough. One of my ministers was known for saying "You help nobody by being poor." This always shocked people. Charles Fillmore, a powerful religious and spiritual teacher, told people that "It is a sin to be poor." Your being poor helps nobody, including yourself.

Being poor does not keep you from helping people or from being a good person. You can still help people when you are poor, but you do it in a much more limited way. When you are poor you can pretty much only help the person in front of you. When you are successful and rich you can help numerous people. Poor people usually cannot donate enough money to build a new wing for a children's hospital. When you are rich, you can donate money that can help children and their families in parts of the world you may never visit. A person with little money may not be able to believe they could ever donate enough money to help build a hospital. The truth is they can. They could go out and solicit funds from rich people and funnel them to the hospital. It would take a huge amount of perseverance, strong communication skills and a commitment to achieve. The belief that they cannot is a small box. On the other hand, dedicating themselves to such a worthy endeavor is a big box.

I dare say there was one person within the last one hundred years who, by outward appearances, seemed to have a small box. This person had a profound effect on the world. She had very few worldly possessions. She slept on the floor and rarely used a mattress. She ate simply. Yet she had a clear mission she was passionately committed to. So much so that she let no one get in her way of doing her good works. Everyone knows what a poor woman Mother Theresa was.

I believed her to be one of the world's richest women, and I mean financially rich. People are astounded when I say this. They saw her living in poverty so that others could be helped. How can I say she was financially wealthy? This "financially poor" woman could make a few phone calls and within an hour have millions of dollars committed to build a charity hospital for the indigent. All she had to do was pick up the phone and call the CEO of a large corporation and tell them she needed money for a hospital or orphanage. Can you imagine anyone saying no to her? She traveled the world and met with presidents and royalty. In her lifetime, she helped more people than live in most large cities.

She set an example and many have followed. Her Sisters of Perpetual Faith still unselfishly help thousands of the poor and sick. Her box was so big and strong that others built their belief based on hers. We tend to take on the beliefs of the people we associate with. We also attract people into our lives based on our beliefs. Have you ever noticed how all the negative people in the office congregate at the same table for lunch? It is easy to see why an optimist with an expanded box would be uncomfortable at a table filled with complaining, limitations, and negativity.

Your job is to become a *Master Box Builder*. You are to be an example for others, practicing positive conversations, and stop the thoughts and actions that are ineffectual. You are to commit to something that is worthy and will bring good to your community and your family. Ask people to join you in this quest. This is one of the best ways to help others build their boxes bigger, better, and stronger.

## Be Present with People

It is a huge gift to be totally present with someone in the moment. In this age of information with the Internet, cell phones, and two hundred TV channels to choose from, we are easily distracted. Often our conversations are stymied and hindered by multi-tasking AND being in a conversation.

Powerful and creative conversations need focus. Have you ever been in conversation with someone who never took his or her eyes away from yours and was excited about what you were saying? Did you feel appreciated and acknowledged? Was there something you really liked about them but couldn't quite identify? What you liked was being treated like a valued and worthy person. They paid attention to you.

We love people who pay attention to us. We love it when they tell us how good we look or how happy they are to see us. Not to compare people to dogs (well, maybe for just a moment), but have you ever noticed how much we like it when dogs get so excited when they see us? Our hearts jump with joy because the dog is literally jumping with enthusiasm just because we are there. One way to inspire people to build a bigger box is to be truly excited when we are with them and to give our full attention to them. And when you are with them, to really be with them.

When you talk to someone, stop and look him or her in the eyes and be present with them. Hold your box (belief) about them that they are important, loved, and appreciated. They will unconsciously pick up on this and they can then expand their box based on your idea of their box. Remember, whether you like it or not, your conversations are steeped in your beliefs about them and they pick up on it. People know if you don't like them or are judging them. They also know if you think they are wonderful and capable just by your conversation with them. They can see your cards, so to speak, through your eyes, tone of voice, and the words you choose.

If you appreciate them and encourage them, you are showing them an expanded box that they can build for themselves. You, however, get to experience the box first. People who are what I call "walking talking encouragers" are magnets for success. Everyone wants to be around them and play on a team with them. They have deep and numerous friendships both socially and in business. A *Master Box Builder* always looks for and finds the good within others. A *Master Box Builder* finds out what is important to others and encourages them to succeed. A *Master Box Builder* has compassionate conversations that are focused and free of distractions.

**Ideas for helping people Build Bigger Boxes:**
1. Build your own box big as an example to others.
2. Appreciate and acknowledge people as often as possible.
3. Be present and actively listen when in a conversation.
4. Know their goals and dreams.
5. Be a partner in helping them achieve their goals.
6. Focus your conversations on success and possibilities.
7. Accept them for who they are.
8. Just love them, really sincerely love them.

# Chapter 6
# **How to Never Worry Again**

## **What, Me Worry?**

There is a simple way of building a box so big that you will never have to worry again. The time and effort we waste worrying is astronomical and the price we pay in ill health and confusion is high. This became evident to me when I was worrying about money a few years ago. I would stay awake at night thinking of the scenarios that might play out with the credit card companies and the mortgage company. I would go over them time and time again in my mind causing myself to lose sleep. These sleepless nights began to show in my health, and frame of mind. The worry never solved my money problems.

After too many nights of this, I decided something had to change. One night, frustrated again by worry, I asked myself if 3:00am was a good time to try to solve this problem. The obvious answer was no. So, I decided to take responsibility and think about it tomorrow at noon, which would be a more reasonable time to solve the problem. This was an intelligent decision, but it was not enough. The worry problem kept popping back into my mind and I would find myself thinking about it. I would eventually catch myself and say "Stop" again only to start up a minute or two later because I had not replaced the negative thought process with a positive one.

The next day, I took a hard look at the situation and realized that 90% of my worry was based in a future which had not, and probably would not, happen. Since the worry was about the future, and the future is not real yet, I decided to just make up another future. In reality, we have only right now, this moment. The future is not real yet, the past is only a memory that we have a story about, there is only now. In the now we can have thoughts about the future, and these thoughts do, in some ways, influence what will happen. So, in the now, I could make up a whole new future. This new future would not be real, except in the new future I would be fabulously wealthy. So I came up with the fantasy of being on a cruise ship.

I had never been on a cruise ship, but I had seen the Love Boat and had an idea that it would be a fun adventure. Whenever I thought about the money problem, the worry scenario would come back; so I would say "Stop" and begin to see myself on a beautiful cruise ship sitting by the pool soaking in the warm rays of the sun. With joy and delight, I would picture the cruise staff bringing me cold sliced fruit as I relaxed by the pool. Continuing with the fantasy story, I would see myself at dinner feasting on a gourmet meal and dancing for hours afterward. Everyone wanted to dance with me because I was funny, witty, and charming. It was a wonderful fantasy. Deep down, I knew neither the worry nor the cruise ship fantasy was real in the moment, but I slept better at night when I thought about the cruise ship. My mind needed something to take the place of the worry.

It was interesting how quickly the money situation cleared up once I quit worrying about it and began responsibly taking care of it at a more appropriate time. The real success came when a friend called a few months later to say he had a "steal of a deal" on a cruise! Since the money situation had cleared up, I could afford it and I went. When I was on the ship, I found myself actually sitting by the pool when the waiters came by with a tray of cold sliced fruit. I smiled to myself and let it be a gentle reminder of how very powerful the mind's thinking abilities can be.

I was not intentionally trying to create a cruise ship experience. I just wanted to stop worrying. Knowing something about how the brain works, I knew I had to replace the worry with something else to concentrate on, so I built a box that had a cruise ship in it. A pretty big box wouldn't you say? There is no limit on how big the box can be.

## The Anatomy of Worry

Worry is the idea of a negative future you make up based on what you perceive to be true. The future is not real, as it has not happened yet. However, as you think about this future, that is not real, your body reacts just as if it were real. It is similar to watching a movie. When you go to a scary movie, you scream and tense your body at the shocking scenes. You know the movie is not real, but your mind and body react as if it were real.

The movie is only colorful light beams dancing on a white screen. The pictures are not real. Not only that, the people in the movie are actors being paid to act, which is not real. With these two very unreal activities (the light beams and the actors) your brain and body treat the movie as if it were genuine and your body reacts accordingly. Horror movies, you could say are doubly unreal and yet we have terrific reactions to them. This makes little rational sense.

You do the same in your own mind for good or for detriment all the time. A fun thought process like the cruise fantasy creates good feelings and the worry process creates bad feelings. You get to choose your thoughts just like when you go to a video store to rent a movie. When you are at the video store you have a multitude of choices like comedy, drama, horror, and travel. After renting the movie, you take it home and pop it in the VCR. The movie plays, your mind responds, and feelings are produced. It is a very simple process. Don't you carefully choose the movies you plan to watch?

So, if the movie playing in your mind is not in alignment with your goals or if it is making you uncomfortable, scared, or stressed, CHANGE IT! Choose a different movie. Your brain is like the VCR, if you don't like the movie, take the tape out and play a new one. Based on my results, I might suggest a movie about a cruise ship.

# Chapter 7
# **Goal Setting**

## Goal Setting

*Master Box Builders* are goal setters. They know the importance of setting goals and they use them as a powerful tool. Goals are ideas and dreams that you desire to be, do, or have in life. Take this chapter very seriously, as if your future counted on it, because it does.

There are five steps to goal setting that have been taught for years. They have been proven to be successful and worthy of your time. Five basic steps that anyone, everyone, can follow.

### Step Number One
### Be Specific

First, be clear about what you want in your life. Make your goals crystal clear and make them measurable. A goal of "more money" is not a clear goal. Receiving five cents could satisfy that goal. Losing one ounce from your mid section would satisfy an unclear goal of "to lose weight." How much more money do you want? Exactly how many pounds do you want to weigh? The goal of having an income of $9,000.00 a month is a clear goal. Wanting to weigh 135 pounds is a clear goal. Be specific.

No one in his or her right mind walks into a grocery store, hands the cashier a $50 bill and an empty bag, and asks them to fill it with groceries. This would most likely not get you the food items you desire. You go to the store with a list (if you remembered to take it off the refrigerator), and go through the aisles retrieving the items that correspond to your list. If you forget to make a list, it becomes a memory game where confusion and distraction rear their ugly heads.

This is similar to life when you have not clearly defined and listed your goals. Not having clear goals certainly blows you off course.

## I Don't Want That

Many people can talk at length about what they specifically do NOT want. Unfortunately, this only produces more of what is not wanted. What we focus our attention on expands or is attracted into our lives. The thought of losing weight only leads people to concentrate on the excess weight they do not want. Look in the mirror and tell yourself what you see. (I know, how cruel). Go ahead and do it anyway. Look in the mirror and you will probably start looking at what is wrong and what you do not want. That wrinkle, this sag, or that love handle. These thoughts will not help you get what you want and they wreak havoc on your self-esteem.

What you focus your attention on is what you get more of. Telling yourself about all the stuff you do not want brings it closer to you. For instance, think about a person who goes to get some ice cream. Most people love ice cream. They go to an ice cream store that has thirty-two flavors. They walk up to the counter and the clerk behind the counter asks what flavor they would like.

If they are the type of person who is always focused on what they do not want in life then the reply goes something like this: 'Well, I don't like that one.' The clerk asks again what flavor they would like. Then they go into how that one over there with nuts tastes really awful. So the clerk asks again what flavor they would like. They then point to another flavor and say how it made them sick one time. Exasperated, the clerk finally explodes with a 'Just tell me what you want and quit telling me what you don't want.'

I guess through the process of elimination, they would eventually get to a flavor they liked. But wouldn't it be easier to simply overlook the ones they do not like and focus on the ones they like? By looking and speaking negatively about the ones they do not like, they are focusing their energy there. This is an energy that creates resistance and bad feelings in their body. The universe deals in a very fair way with people who stay focused on what they do not want; they get more of it.

## Positive and Affirmative
When setting your goals, state them in the affirmative, focusing on what you do want. Avoid using words such as try, want, and if. The goal of losing 20 pounds is focusing on what you don't want. You don't want the 20 pounds. What you really want is to weigh 135 pounds, or to wear a size 8 dress, or have a 32-inch waist. This is focusing on what you want.

There is a different feeling when you are focusing on what you want. Check it out for yourself. Think about wanting to lose 20 pounds. How do you feel about the 20 pounds that you do not want? Look at the weight and see what kind of thoughts come up for you. Not too many people can look at their love handles or thighs and feel really good about them. What they want is the weight to be gone. They don't want it. How do you feel when you don't want something? Resistant! Resistance does not bring good feelings.

How about seeing yourself weighing exactly what you want? How about seeing your body in the right proportions? Think about how good you would feel in that certain dress or waist size. Now this brings good feelings.

You are more apt to achieve a goal when focused on what you want which produces good feelings.

We have been taught the opposite over the years. So it is up to us to change our thinking and beliefs – to expand the box. By the way, it is not the weight we really want to lose, it is the feeling we think we are going to get when we step on the scales and a certain number appears. Earlier in the book we covered this. Fantasize your goal already achieved and create the desired feeling. You do not need the outcome to feel the desired feeling. It is so much harder achieving the goal with the mindset of 'I will feel better once I accomplish the goal.' Achieve the goal in your mind and let those feelings propel your action in working for the goal.

## What if I'm Wrong?

Some people may not want to be clear about their goals for fear that something better might come along they have not thought about. Or, what if they pick the wrong goal? What if they fail? Or what if some people think they are greedy. What if, what if, what if? Stop that right now and just pick something.

**Be specific with the following criteria:**
1. Is it clear and definable?
2. On what date do you want it realized?
3. Will it bring a better life for you and your family?
4. Is it in alignment with your values?
5. Will it bring you a deep sense of fulfillment, joy, or peace?
6. Does it stir up inner passion and excitement?
7. Are you truly interested in it?
8. Would you be willing to go the extra mile to achieve it?

## Step Number Two
### Write Your Goals Down

This is a crucial and very important step. Less than 5% of Americans actually have their goals written down on paper. In a class I taught recently, a gentleman stood up and told me he did not need to write his goals down because he kept them right smack in the middle of his brain. It took a great deal of restraint for me not to blurt out that this was exactly where they were probably going to stay. You cannot build a beautiful home with the drawings residing solely in your mind. A necessary element of achieving your goals is to put them on the drawing board and plan them in writing.

While goals always begin in your mind, to become reality, they must be put into a physical form. Writing them down is a crucial part of the process. They may need fine-tuning and bolstering and writing helps in that process. The writing process involves using the sense of sight and touch. The more senses you use when focusing on your goals, the better they are stored in your memory.

## Step Number Three
### Put a Time on Your Goals

There are so many choices. Short-term, long-term, medium-term. Which is best? They are all appropriate. If you need to, begin with some short-term goals. Set some goals for the next one to three months. You could even set goals for one week at a time, but you probably can go out to three months to a year. Whatever goals you set, make them achievable in the time allotted. Tripling your income or losing 100 pounds in the next thirty days is not believable and most likely not going to happen. You may really desire it, but why set yourself up for failure?

Here is a loose outline for short-term, medium-term and long- term goals. Short-term goals are from one month to one year. Medium-term would be one to ten years. Long term goals are from ten to a hundred years. A hundred years??? The Japanese literally set fifty and one hundred year goals.

If you think about it, this is not as ludicrous as it sounds. In our lifetime, we have seen the average life span continue to increase. With all the medical breakthroughs we experience these days, we are most likely going to see healthier people living into the hundreds. We would do well planning to be busy into our nineties. Can you imagine retiring at 65 and doing very little until the age of 115? Sitting around doing little for fifty years does not sound like fun. Use your imagination for a moment. Wouldn't it be great to have three full careers in a lifetime? For your first twenty years be a teacher or a bartender, then the next twenty years be a golf pro or a pilot, and then for the last twenty years be a professor or an investment banker. Oh the things we can do, if we plan and dream now.

### Step Number Four
#### Read them Twice a Day

The best way to stay on track and focused is to read your goals twice every day. A good time to read them is in the morning and then again before bed. It is a superb way of starting your day and an even better way to send you off to sleep.

In today's society, we are bombarded with information from all kinds of sources like people, TV, radio, billboards, and the internet, to name just a few. Many people are in information overload and can be easily influenced off course. What to do? Sailors continually check their compass to ensure they are on course. Boats, like people, tend to drift off course a little each day.

Captains make adjustments in their headings based on where they are and where they want to go. They do this several times each day. You too, need to check your goals each day take an honest look at where you are and make the appropriate adjustments to achieve the desired results.
When reviewing your goals each day, read them out loud with feeling. Years of studying effective learning methods have revealed that the more people use the five senses, the better they retain the information. By reading your goals out loud everyday you are building new belief systems, i.e., bigger boxes.

This step also includes getting into the feeling of already having, doing, or being the goal. Remember that the imagination falls into the mental realm. This is not enough. You must also use your feeling nature in conjunction with your mental nature. Using only the mental or only the emotional realms will produce spotty results and achieving the goal may take much longer. Say your goals out loud, in the affirmative, generating feelings.

## Step Number Five
### Take Action
This step may sound daunting, but don't let it. As a matter of fact, most of the steps you need to take to reach your goals are going to be small daily actions. How do you get to the top of the mountain? Make sure every step you take is toward the top of the mountain, and take them one step at a time.

Direction, steadfastness, and perseverance are the keys. Think about daily actions, small daily actions that will add up to big results. The way to build a wall is placing one brick at a time on the wall. Just keep putting up the bricks.

Our society has created the illusion that the things we want can all happen in an instant. One kiss from the prince and the princess awakens. Rub a lamp, and poof, a genie pops out. One strike in the ground with a pick ax and up comes a bubbling crude, black gold with the mansion in Beverly Hills. Wonderful, extraordinary things can happen in a flash, but most likely they will come from daily tasks that lead to accomplished goals.

After setting your goals, it is crucial to take the steps to achieve them. If people don't take the necessary steps they set themselves up for failure. Let's say that you want to lose weight. You might sit down and write out exactly how much you would like to weigh and in what time frame. Make a game plan. If you do not take the planned daily actions that are in alignment with the goal, your success may elude you.

By writing down the goal you are making a commitment to yourself. However, if your actions are in opposition to the goal, you are breaking your commitment to yourself. This is called a "breach of integrity." How do you feel when people are showing no integrity when dealing with you? Well, the same holds true in your relationship with yourself. Most people go into denial regarding breaking their word to themselves, in this case not following the goal up with action. Still, they have broken their word to themselves and at some internal level they will feel guilty, angry and or frustrated.

Knowing what your goals are will not be enough. Knowing how to fish does not put fish in the frying pan. Action is vital. Any action, as long as it is in alignment with the goal. Just keep doing the actions that are intelligent and that are in front of you. Small tasks lead you to achieved goals. Make doing the tasks a fun and enjoyable journey.

## Goal Setting Review

1. <u>Be Specific</u>
   - Set clear goals you desire.
   - Focus on what you want.
   - Write them in the affirmative.
2. <u>Write Your Goals Down</u>
   - Write them with pen and paper.
3. <u>Put a Time on Your Goals</u>
   - Short-term.
   - Medium-term.
   - Long-term.
4. <u>Read Them Twice a Day</u>
   - Read them out loud.
5. <u>Take Action</u>
   - Take small steps every day.
   - Set up a support system to hold yourself accountable and on track.

## Get your Paper

This is an action step. Focus on some short-term goals to make your start. Write down two or three goals for each of the following areas: physical health, mental and emotional well being, family, finances, spiritual, and your relationship to society. Don't go overboard; just write down three desirable goals for each area. This is when you want to set the book down and go get a pen and some paper. Remember, Action!

You should now have quite a few goals on paper. Now, write out three reasons or "whys" you want the goals. This creates passion and desire. Next, write down three things you can do on a daily basis to achieve your goals. Examples:

Goal:
*I now weigh 135 pounds on or before September 1ˢᵗ.*
  <u>Whys</u>:
    1. To look better.
    2. To feel better.
    3. So I can feel great wearing a size 6 dress or having a 32-inch waist.

  <u>Actions</u>:
    1. Take the stairs at work.
    2. Replace unhealthy food at home with tasty healthy food.
    3. Drink 8 glasses of water every day instead of sodas.

**<u>Goal</u>:**
*I now make $9,000.00 a month by December 1ˢᵗ.*
  <u>Whys</u>:
    1. So I can have a healthy retirement account.
    2. We can take wonderful vacations every year.
    3. To have the ability to pay off my credit card bills.
  <u>Actions</u>:
    1. Read this goal twice a day with feeling.
    2. Be open to new ways of bringing in money.
    3. Make ten sales calls each day.

Get the idea? Another variable on this is to write down three negative things you are currently doing in regards to the goal. Immediately turn around and write out new behaviors that would be in alignment with the goal. Then scratch out the negative.

Example:

*I now weigh 135 pounds on or before September 1ˢᵗ.*

Old action: Drinking 4 sodas each day.
New action: I drink 8 glasses of water every day.

Old Action: Snacking on chips and cookies.
New Action: I eat carrot sticks and other healthy snacks.

Old action: Watching too much TV.
New action: I go for a walk and exercise each day.

Don't just quit negative behaviors. This is not enough. It helps to replace the negative behaviors with supportive behaviors. If you are used to eating cookies every afternoon and try to stop, you are going to notice something missing. That is when you will need an activity to immediately replace the old behavior. Planning ahead is crucial. People are creatures of habit and old habits can come back if they are not replaced.

## Treasure Map

Another tool helpful in setting and reaching goals is called a treasure map, life cycle plan, or dream chart. It is a collage of pictures depicting the kind of life you want to live. Goal setting must be clear and a treasure map embodies that element beautifully. After you have written out your goals and they are clear, it is time to start looking through magazines.

Creating a treasure map is simple. Cut out pictures from magazines that represent your goals and values. You may even want to include photographs of friends and family. Pictures of houses, and cars, and beautiful clothes are a part of the treasure map. You can even put in words, phrases, poems, or scripture. The desired result is a treasure map that generates a sense of joy and happiness when you look at it.

To make the project fun, I recommend that you do this with someone else or with a group of others. Have some food and drinks and turn this into a banquet of goal setting. Bring in lots and lots of various magazines, scissors, poster board, and glue. Play some uplifting music and start looking through the magazines. Clip out pictures that represent your goals and values. Use your creativity and imagination in this process.

Let the others know the types of pictures you are looking for and you can help each other in the search. This makes it fun and everyone can support each other in the goal setting process.

Be specific about what you place on the treasure map. If you want a red Lincoln Navigator then don't put a blue Chevy truck on it. Go to the car dealership and get a brochure that has the exact make, model, and color you desire. It would be remarkable if you actually found the car and had the salesman take a picture of you sitting in the driver's seat. What a great picture to place on your treasure map!

You may also want to find a picture of yourself that you particularly like. Maybe one of you smiling, or doing something you love, or one where you just plain look good. Paste this in the middle of the treasure map so when you look at it you can see yourself surrounded by the incredible life you have constructed on the treasure map.

You do not have to limit the pictures to just goals. You can also represent your values like honesty, family, religion/spirituality, volunteering, environment, etc. Include your purpose and mission statement on the treasure map. Having a nice home and a beautiful car is good, but they are not the source of your happiness. Your inner values bring the happiness and joy to your life. This is the place to showcase them.

I have seen people paste a picture of a pack of cigarettes with a big red X on it or a credit card bill with "Paid in Full." You can add pictures of praying hands, laughing children, a sunset, and even a picture of an incredible body with a picture of your own head pasted on it. Remember, be creative and have fun.

Once you have finished, place the treasure map somewhere you can look at it each day. There are a number of effective daily uses for the treasure map. Remember, this is a tool to help clarify your goals and to magnetize them to you. You can take the treasure map to a local copy center and have it laminated. Why laminate it? So you can put it in the shower and see your incredible life while washing away the old you. You can also place it on the wall by your bed so it is the first thing you see when you awaken and the last thing you see before you go to bed.

One of my students placed hers by her desk to remind her of her incredible life. She acts as if it is already true. As she makes sales and business calls, this rallies her to good feelings. If she has a call that goes less than expected, she says 'so what,' and turns to look at the treasure map and to affirm her incredible life. This refocuses her energy for the next call.

I have a rule that whenever I pass my treasure map I must touch one of the pictures and then laugh. This encompasses the senses of sight, touch, and sound. The laughter is a happy feeling I generate while looking at a clear picture. This may sound like an unusual practice, but it goes along with everything this book teaches. Have a clear goal (the picture), be committed to it (daily action), and have passion (the feeling). To more effectively and quickly create the kind of life you say you want, include your mind and heart, your thoughts/beliefs, and your feelings.

Clear Goal > Feeling/Passion > Action > Result

## Motivate Me, Please!

Your goals are your greatest motivating factor. Your commitment and persistence in your daily actions produce results. With your goals written down, you can begin to compare them to your conversations each day. Ask, "Does this conversation support me in achieving my goals?" Reading goals aloud is a conversation you have with yourself which in turn creates a bigger box in which to live. Looking at your treasure map and touching a picture while laughing is another conversation with yourself. Writing goals on paper is also a conversation. Conversations change your life. Be sure your conversations regarding your goals create big boxes.

## Create a Dream Team

Do not tell everyone you know what your goals are. People tend to play the devil's advocate and point out shortcomings, faults, and problems. They think this is helping you or they may just be pessimists. You do not need them throwing small boxes at you by telling you their opinions or beliefs.

Do you think Thomas Edison listened to all the people who told him that using electricity was impossible or evil while he invented the first light bulb?  Do you think listening to these people helped him in the process?  If you are running a marathon do you want the fans on the sidelines to yell how tired and exhausted you look?  Personally I want them yelling how good I am doing regardless of how I look.

A good rule of thumb is to share your goals with no more than three people.  Find a mentor or coach who can see the possibilities, not the limitations.  Family members, while they love you, may want to be "helpful" by pointing out your limitations.  Why?  They know you, all of you, good and bad.  They say things like, 'Okay honey, I want to help you lose weight, but you have tried so many times and failed.  And you know how much you love cookies.  But if you really want to lose weight, I will try to help you.'  You may need to teach them about creating big boxes.

Prayer partners are a grand idea.  Adding the spiritual foundation of your religion to your goals is a powerful bonus.  Make sure that if you pray on a regular basis with a selective group that you leave all other conversations at the door.  Do not pray and then talk about how hard it is or that you are not seeing any progress.  This negates the prayers.  Pray with faith and let your conversations, all conversations, be in alignment with the goals as answered prayers.  See it already completed.  See the fields already ripe with the harvest, even if it is winter.  Seeing is believing.  Believing in the possibilities and taking action is crucial to manifesting your goals.  Remember, when you pray, move your feet.

### Goal Card
Another way to stay aware of your goals is to carry a goal card in your pocket.  This is simply a card about the size of a regular business card, on which you have written your top three goals.  Keep this card in your pocket or purse or

organizer. This way it is always with you. The rule is: whenever you touch it or physically see it, you must read it. Each time you reach in your pocket and you touch it, the goal card is to be taken out and read. You may read it thirty or forty times a day. Reading it out loud is best as it helps you to be clearly focused and creates the feeling of the goal being achieved.

When you take the card out and read it, take a moment to feel the goal as already achieved. Really take a moment and concentrate on it. See the goal already manifested and feeling as if it were already a done deal. Again, this is where you bring your mind and heart together. Seeing in your mind the finished result and creating the feeling of the goal realized. Do not underestimate the power of this technique.

Many people get the goal card laminated at a local copy center. The goal card will hold up much better this way. You want it to look good and be something you like holding in your hand. A flimsy piece of paper will not last long enough for this use. You may want to print it on a special paper in a nice type before you have it laminated.

# Chapter 8
# Staying Above the Line

## Float Your Cork

Imagine a cork in water. What is the natural state of a cork in relation to water? Floating and bobbing on top, right? Can the cork be pulled below the line? Certainly. Can it be held there for long periods of time? Of course. What happens if you let go and stop holding it down? It floats right back up to the top, above the water line to the surface. It requires energy to hold the cork down underneath the water where it is below its natural state.

Imagine you are the cork. Your natural state is to be above the line, floating on the top. When you are floating you feel good. When you are underneath the water you do not feel so good. When you find yourself under the water line, what is the energy or force that has pulled you down below your natural, happy state?

Study the illustration below. Our cork, in its natural state, is anywhere above the line. The activities below the line are the mechanisms we use to hold our cork below the line.

Feelings of Love, Peace, Happiness,
Freedom, Clarity, Health
**ABOVE THE LINE**

Resentment
Revenge
Blame
Being Right
Complaining
Resistance
Condemnation and Judgment

## Definitions of "Below the Line":

Resentment – This is re-felt anger. You get angry with a person or situation and then don't let it go for weeks, months, or even years. A sure sign of resentment is if you are re-telling the same story over and over and the old feelings are reactivated.

Revenge – This is a dangerous activity with the same results as a boom-a-rang. There are two spiritual laws that exemplify this "What I do to my brother, I do to myself," and "What goes around, comes around."

Blame – This is not taking responsibility for your own actions or results; blaming other people and situations for the unfortunate circumstances of your life. When you are pointing your finger at others, you always have three pointing back at you.

Being Right – This is more of an attitude of living life with all the answers. Knowing better than others and making sure others know when and how they are wrong or mistaken. Also included is not being open to answers from other people.

Complaining – Complaining is often justified as being "realistic." It includes expressing resentment and dissatisfaction. It is a conversation that produces negative feelings in yourself and in others. It is a "victim" conversation.

Resistance – This is any form of non-acceptance. Situations you do not like or think should be some other way will bring up resistance. When you focus on what you don't like or don't want, you get more of that.

<u>Condemnation and Judgment</u> – This is looking at life situations as either bad or wrong based on your belief systems. Many of the judgments you make on a daily basis are over small things. But they add up quickly and carry a hefty price tag.

The price you pay for these negative activities is living below the line. Some of the results of being below the line may be: poor health, conflict, discord, dis-ease, poor relationships, anger, pain, carelessness, inattention, indifference.

When you stop dragging your cork under the water, you can begin to feel the joy of living again. The key here is knowing when you are holding your cork below the line, and knowing when you are harboring and nurturing a resentment. Know when you are blaming others rather than looking in the mirror and taking responsibility. Some people have been holding the cork under the water for so long, they don't even know they are wet. Being wet feels normal for them. How sad! Think about what that continues to attract.

Feeling anger and resentment only attracts more of the same. You are a magnet that attracts situations that correspond to the feelings and beliefs you hold. Remember that happy people attract other happy people. Angry, negative people attract angry, negative people. This cycle must be broken. Awareness is the first step. With it comes the choice to change. Without awareness, nothing changes.

Being aware you are in resentment is important. One way to discover if you are in resentment is to notice if you are telling an anger story that is more than a year old. For example, you remember 10 years ago that Aunt Jane put pecans in the Jell-O at the family reunion and she knew you were allergic. Get over it and stop telling the story. Telling it one more time is not going to help. It only generates feelings that do nothing for your good health and peace of mind.

Hey, what about forgiving her? What a novel idea! Maybe in a moment of anger she said she did not care if you got any Jell-O and put in the pecans. Maybe she was having a tough day and forgot about your allergy. Maybe she honestly forgot and then realized it too late and she has felt awful for years. Maybe it was her Jell-O mold, but she did not actually make it. Who knows? It doesn't matter. What matters is that you are holding on to resentments and it is time to let them go or you will continue to live with their offensive awful gifts.

There is a bill that must be paid when you pull your cork under the water. The amount to be paid goes up everyday the cork is held under the water. Let the cork float and the debt is nullified. Debt is only part of the price that must be paid, there is also lasting damage.

## Prices you pay for living below the line:

| | |
|---|---|
| Poor health | Loss of time |
| Conflict | Restricted Growth |
| Discord | Loss of credibility |
| Dis-ease | Insomnia |
| Poor relationships | Jail |
| Anger | Lose-lose situations |
| Pain | Depression |
| Carelessness | Frustration |
| Inattention | Alienation |
| Indifference | Loss of direction & Focus |
| Guilt | Loss of opportunities |

What happens when we let go of the negative and let the cork float? A whole new change occurs within our minds and bodies. It is as if sunlight blasts through our body and a sense of freedom and happiness is reestablished. Below are a number of the positive results that are restored.

### Payoffs you receive for "Floating Your Cork":

| | |
|---|---|
| Peace of mind | Opportunity |
| Good health | Growth |
| Contentment | Respect |
| Fulfillment | Admiration |
| Success | Money |
| Positive attitude | Connectedness |
| High energy | Freedom |
| Better relationships | Win-Win |
| Clear focus | Optimism |
| Intuition | |

So how does a person float their cork? Deliberate action. Again, first you must know that your cork is under the water where it does not belong. A quick gauge is to check and see how you feel. If you feel any of the negative experiences outlined above, then your cork is probably submerged and needs to be floated. Below is an excellent list of activities that will assist you in floating your cork and keeping it above the line.

## Techniques to "Float Your Cork" and "Stay Above the Line":

Forgiveness

Prayer

Therapy

Praise others

Ask for help

Hug someone

Be accountable

Listen

Be humble

Humor

Take a deep breath

Create a vision

Look for good in others

Turn the other cheek

Admit when wrong

Talk & communicate

Say thank you

Read good stuff

Create a bigger box

Close your mouth

Count to 10

Write in a journal

Exercise

Send out positive thoughts

Love self

Self care

Open-mindedness

Practice your values

Dodge small boxes

Play with your dog or cat

## Putting it into Practice

Most of the activities to get your cork floating are easily understandable AND you already know them. They are not foreign to you. So why isn't our cork floating all the time? We know what to do. It is because there is a big difference between knowing what to do and actually doing it. Let me give you an example. There are three frogs on a log. One decides to jump off. How many frogs are now on the log? Three. Why? The one frog only decided, he did not jump. A decision is different than actually doing it.

Given time, I would hope the frog would jump off the log after the decision. But like people, it does not always happen. Action is the key to your transformation. Knowing how to play golf and actually playing golf are two completely different things. Joining a Health Club is different than actually going and working out and doing aerobics. Just because you pay dues each month does not mean you are getting any healthier or thinner.

Consciously thinking about the techniques to stay above the line is a start. Take one or two each day and focus on doing them. Practice them until they are second nature in your daily interactions with yourself and others.

# Chapter 9

# Twenty-one Days to Becoming a
## *Master Box Builder*

### Practice, Practice, Practice
Now it is time to actually take the teachings of this book and apply them to your life. The following twenty-one day program is designed to be simple and effective in changing your box size. The lessons are easy to do and can be done throughout the day. Start the day by reading the lesson and writing a few notes on how you can best implement it. Before you retire at night, write out some of your thoughts from the day's exercise.

Now, go build a bigger, better box.

## Day 1

**<u>Be Aware of Your Feelings</u>**

Today, become aware of your box size. Regularly check how your body is feeling. Take note of when you are feeling stress or feeling happy. This day is focused on being aware of your current box size in regards to your feelings and emotions. Begin to picture your box in reference to your feelings. Today, build a big box by generating good feelings.

Morning Ideas

_____

_____

_____

_____

_____

_____

Evening Notes

_____

_____

_____

_____

_____

_____

## Be Aware of Your Thinking

Today, be aware of your box size that is connected to your thoughts and thinking patterns. See how often the old negative thinking patterns reveal themselves. Say "Stop," and do one of the exercises that have been suggested in this book to expand your box. Notice how optimistic thoughts create a flow in your life and how pessimistic thoughts create resistance and unfavorable feelings.

Morning Ideas

_____

_____

_____

_____

_____

_____

Evening Notes

_____

_____

_____

_____

_____

_____

# Day 3

## Be Aware of your Conversations

Pay special attention to the words you speak today. Listen to yourself as you speak to people. The words you speak have power. Today, notice if you are using any negative language, justifications, complaining, or words of anger. Be attentive to how your positive conversations with others raise your energy level.

Morning Ideas

_____

_____

_____

_____

_____

_____

Evening Notes

_____

_____

_____

_____

_____

_____

## Day 4
### <u>Be Aware of Other People's Box Size</u>

Be the observer today. Take a moment to step back and listen to people's conversations. What are they revealing to you about themselves in the words, sentences, and body language they are projecting? Watch their bodies and notice what happens when they talk in positive and negative ways. Are they being a mirror for you?

Morning Ideas

_____

_____

_____

_____

_____

_____

Evening Notes

_____

_____

_____

_____

_____

_____

## Day 5

**<u>No Complaining Today</u>**

This ought to be fun. No complaining at all, not even if it is justified. Not even if the other person is totally wrong. Don't worry, you can go back to complaining tomorrow (and pay the price), but today no complaining about anything, not even in your thoughts.

Morning Ideas

_____

_____

_____

_____

_____

_____

Evening Notes

_____

_____

_____

_____

_____

_____

## Day 6

### **Rampage of Appreciation for Others**

Today you are to go out and sincerely appreciate people. Tell them you value and admire them. Tell them something you like about them. Pay them a compliment. Do this with your family, co-workers, and anyone you come into contact with. Try it on the grocery store clerk. Sincerity is a must today. Let it come from your heart. Notice how you feel when you acknowledge someone. Does your box get bigger?

Morning Ideas

_____

_____

_____

_____

_____

_____

Evening Notes

_____

_____

_____

_____

_____

_____

## Day 7
### __Rampage of Appreciation for Your Surroundings__

Take several moments today to appreciate everything you see. Include the trees, the clouds, your home, your car, and the streets. Anything you see or come into physical contact with, appreciate it. Use the *Sixteen Seconds for LIFE* process as often as possible today. Look, Interpret as good, Feel it, and Experience it.

Morning Ideas

_____

_____

_____

_____

_____

_____

Evening Notes

_____

_____

_____

_____

_____

_____

## Day 8

### **Rampage of Appreciation for Yourself**

This morning look in the mirror and find five things you like about yourself. Today appreciate yourself, your actions, and your attributes. Give yourself credit for the good you are and the good you are doing. Use the *Sixteen Seconds for LIFE* process as many times as you can today.

Morning Ideas

_____

_____

_____

_____

_____

Evening Notes

_____

_____

_____

_____

_____

## Day 9

### Rampage of Appreciation for Your Job

Love your job today and everyone connected to it. See if you can find something good about your job and appreciate it. Treasure the people you work with and let them know it today. If you want another job, put it on hold for today and simply appreciate the one you have now. Actively disliking your job (focusing on what you do not want) will not help you in getting the job you desire. Today generate some good feelings about your current job situation.

Morning Ideas

_____

_____

_____

_____

_____

_____

Evening Notes

_____

_____

_____

_____

_____

_____

## Day 10
### **Live as if Your Dreams and Goals are Already True**

Play the 100% game today (Chapter 3). Cover the major areas in your life: physical, mental, spiritual, family, society, and finances. This would be a good day to carry your goals around with you so you can reference them. This exercise is for you to do by yourself. At least once today, play the game speaking out loud for 4 minutes. Your drive to work would be a great time.

Morning Ideas

_____

_____

_____

_____

_____

_____

Evening Notes

_____

_____

_____

_____

_____

_____

## Day 11
### Build a Bigger Box about Money

What new belief would you like to have about money? Here are a few ideas: 'Money comes to me easily,' 'There always seems to be plenty of money in my life,' 'Huge amounts of money come in the mail,' 'It feels good to save and invest money,' 'Money comes from my job and multiple other sources.' Pick a new belief you would like to instill in your consciousness and stick with it all day. Write it down and say it out loud. Be sure to feel it as you are saying it.

Morning Ideas

_____

_____

_____

_____

_____

_____

Evening Notes

_____

_____

_____

_____

_____

_____

## Day 12
### Add a New Belief about Yourself

Today is a day for creating a new you. Start this day with some self-appreciation and pick one new opinion of yourself. This idea needs to be about a value or inner characteristic. Ideas: 'I am smart,' 'I think in new and positive ways,' 'My body feels good,' 'I am fulfilled in my relationships with my family.'

Morning Ideas

_____

_____

_____

_____

_____

_____

Evening Notes

_____

_____

_____

_____

_____

_____

## Be Aware of Your Box Size

Now that you have succeeded in finishing twelve days of the program, it is time for another day of awareness. Throughout the day ask yourself how big your box is. Observe your conversations and thinking. Check your feelings and energy levels. Notice the connection between your thinking, conversations, feelings, energy levels, and box size. What is working well for you and what needs to be changed?

Morning Ideas

_____

_____

_____

_____

_____

_____

Evening Notes

_____

_____

_____

_____

_____

_____

## Day 14

**<u>Radical Forgiveness</u>**

The one stumbling block every human being faces is holding on to anger and resentment. It keeps boxes small, limited, and repressed. Today, you are to forgive anyone and anything you have judged. If any resentful thoughts appear, immediately forgive the person or situation and release them to God and or to peace. Active forgiveness is today's project.

Morning Ideas

_____

_____

_____

_____

_____

Evening Notes

_____

_____

_____

_____

_____

## Day 15

### **Deliberate Creation of Joy**

This is your day to deliberately create the feeling of joy. Today's activity is to choose joy over all other feelings. During the day, remind yourself that joy is the intention and have conversations and thoughts that generate joy in your experience. What inner dialogue can help you generate joy? When interacting with others, what conversations produce joy? What activities can you choose in this day to create joy for yourself? Focus on producing the actual feeling in your body of joy.

Morning Ideas

_____

_____

_____

_____

_____

Evening Notes

_____

_____

_____

_____

_____

# Day 16

## Deliberate Creation of Love

Yesterday you created joy; today you are to create love. The first step in creating is intent. Let your intention be love; love in your relationships, love in your work, love in yourself. Interact with people that you love today. Call a friend or family member you love and actively create a feeling of love in your body. Connect with people in such a way that love is the outcome of your conversations with them.

Morning Ideas

_____

_____

_____

_____

_____

_____

Evening Notes

_____

_____

_____

_____

_____

_____

## Day 17

### **Deliberate Creation of Peace**

Today let your intention be to create feelings of peace, harmony, and serenity. A sense of knowing that all is well is your focus today. Stop and reflect several times today on creating peace with your thoughts and actions. Relax and allow yourself to simply be in the flow.

Morning Ideas

_____

_____

_____

_____

_____

_____

Evening Notes

_____

_____

_____

_____

_____

_____

## Day 18
## <u>Conversations about Possibilities and Goodness</u>

Profess words of possibility today in all your conversations. Whenever a new idea arises from you or another person, look for and speak words of encouragement and possibility. Keep saying YES to life and its wonderful unfoldment. Your job is to transform your conversations to what is good and worthy. Today, you are a walking, talking YES to life.

Morning Ideas

_____

_____

_____

_____

_____

_____

Evening Notes

_____

_____

_____

_____

_____

_____

## <u>Dodge Small Boxes</u>

Small boxes are thrown around all day long. They come from: TV, radio, news, family, co-workers, and sometimes friends. They look like negativity, gossip, judgment, and lack. Let them pass without attachment or judgment. If an insult or words of belittlement come your way, know that they are not for you. Simply disregard them and remind yourself of what is true. What is true is that you are a wonderful person living in a world that is making great progress for everyone.

Morning Ideas

_____

_____

_____

_____

_____

_____

Evening Notes

_____

_____

_____

_____

_____

_____

## Day 20

### **Building a Big Box of Gratitude**

Walk in gratitude today. Say thank you for all the good you can find. Take a ten or fifteen minute relaxing walk today and count your blessings. Literally walk and think of the many things you can be grateful for. There are countless wonderful and precious elements in your life. Focus on gratitude and observe your box enlarge. Make a list a few times today of all the good in your life. Take three minutes and write out ten things you are grateful for.

Morning Ideas

_____

_____

_____

_____

_____

_____

Evening Notes

_____

_____

_____

_____

_____

_____

## Consciously Choose a Big Box Today

Today you graduate as a *Master Box Builder*. You have practiced a number of techniques for expanding your box. You have inspired others to enlarge their box. Your question throughout the day is 'How can I enlarge my box in this situation?' Remind yourself as often as possible to build your box bigger.

Morning Ideas

_____

_____

_____

_____

_____

_____

Evening Notes

_____

_____

_____

_____

_____

_____

# Goal Page

**Goal:** _____

_____

**Whys:**

1. _____

2. _____

3. _____

Old Action: _____

*New Action:* _____

Old Action: _____

*New Action:* _____

Old Action: _____

*New Action:* _____

# Goal Page

**Goal:** _____

_____

**Whys:**

4. _____

5. _____

6. _____

Old Action: _____

*New Action:* _____

Old Action: _____

*New Action:* _____

Old Action: _____

*New Action:* _____

# Goal Page

**Goal:** _____

_____

**Whys:**

7. _____

8. _____

9. _____

Old Action: _____

*New Action:* _____

Old Action: _____

*New Action:* _____

Old Action: _____

*New Action:* _____

# Goal Page

**Goal:** _____

_____

**Whys:**

10. _____

11. _____

12. _____

Old Action: _____

*New Action:* _____

Old Action: _____

*New Action:* _____

Old Action: _____

*New Action:* _____

Printed in the United States
28789LVS00007B/34-39

9 780970 681737